MW01046323

A Guide to Dry Stone Walling

A dry stone wall constructed by the author as part of an agricultural enclosure.

A dry stone retaining wall serving as a useful garden feature., also built by the author.

A Guide to
Dry Stone Walling

Andy Radford

The Crowood Press

First published in 2001 by
The Crowood Press Ltd
Ramsbury, Marlborough
Wiltshire SN8 2HR

British Library Cataloguing-in-Publication Data
A catalogue record for this book is available from the British
Library.

ISBN 1 86126 444 5

Acknowledgements
I would like to thank those individuals and organizations that
have been supportive throughout the writing of this book. Janet
Williams for proofreading and making coffee. Vivian and all the
staff at the Berwyn Slate Quarry, who supplied the stone for many
of the projects featured herein. Robert Hill for his valuable help
with the construction of the batter frames. Geraint, Kate and
Harry Jones of Pant Dafydd Goch, Eifion and Carys Davies of
Pantddu Farm near Llangollen, Sue and Paul Lewis from Dinbren
Hall and Bill Hardy, Arthur Hardy and Gill Parry of Pen y Gaer
Farm, Garth, whose walls are featured in this book. Pete
Hardwick, Pam Pickering, Bob Young and Terry Page of the Peak
District National Park Ranger Service with whom I enjoyed a day
out with conservation volunteers. North Shropshire and Walford
College, Shropshire for permission to photograph their dry stone
wall. The Dartmoor National Park Authority, the Lake District
National Park Authority, the BTCV, the Dry Stone Walling
Association for invaluable support and a special thank you to
Roger Gardener who helped build the walls.

Typeset by Carreg Limited, Ross-on-Wye, Herefordshire

Printed and bound in Great Britain by Bookcraft Limited

CONTENTS

PREFACE

Dry stone walling is the oldest and most versatile of all countryside crafts. Without the use of mortar, the ancient inhabitants of the British Isles constructed their dwellings, municipal buildings and later boundaries using the odd-shaped stones lifted from the ground.

I first became interested in the craft as a child, driving through the Peak District National Park on days out with my parents. I spent a great deal of time observing the complex structures that criss-crossed the hillsides. How were they built? Why don't they fall down? Are you sure they don't need cement? No one could answer my questions. I must have made a conscious effort then to get to the bottom of this mystery, for I eventually achieved employment with the Peak District National Park Authority. I will be forever indebted to the staff of the Peak Park Joint Planning Board. It was through their comprehensive training programmes that I became competent at this and other rural crafts. I have this organization to thank for the skills I now possess, and the knowledge that enabled me to write this book.

Amongst other things I have been building dry stone walls for sixteen years and now run a landscape business in North Wales. I'm still building walls, but I have exchanged the majestic fells of the Peak district for the beautiful Berwyn Mountains near Llangollen. Much of my work involves the repair and reconstruction of walls that were originally built hundreds of years ago. As I practise my trade with the backdrop of the mythical Grail castle of Dinas Bran, I often wonder if, in the castle's heyday, a viewer from the battlements then might have gazed upon a stockman doing exactly the same thing all those years ago.

CHAPTER 1

INTRODUCTION

One of the most striking features of the British landscape is the unending file of dry stone walls criss-crossing our upland, pastures and ascending moorland and fell. Many have stood for hundreds of years, buffeted and scarred by an unyielding barrage of rain, wind and snow, and still stand proud and strong to this day; monuments made from simple architectural techniques. An accolade to those craftsmen who struggled to climb the steepest incline carrying stone and tools, braving the elements day in, day out.

The actual art of dry stone walling dates back thousands of years and the Celts were absolute masters of the craft. Evidence of their skill can still be seen today with their intricately constructed cells within the British Isles. Perhaps the most striking element of this skill is that the technique has not really changed and the walls constructed today employ the very same principles used by those ancient tribes. When the landscape was initially populated more than 4,000 years ago, the tribes were hunter-gatherers and did not practise agriculture. Most of the remains of their architecture have revealed to historians that their dry stone buildings were used for dwellings and ceremonial purposes. There are many Stone Age examples of the use of dry stone construction; hut circles in

Dartmoor, and burial mounds in the North and South Downs are some of the best. Later tribes built barrows and cairns, many of these can be seen on the upland areas of Britain. Iron Age Celts built homes using natural stone; some agricultural enclosures were constructed at this time. In the far North of Scotland, on the Isles of Hebrides and Orkney, there are examples of villages constructed from natural stones. One of the most striking features is the 'Brochs'; possibly used for ceremonial purposes, these are tall cylindrical towers built of dry stones.

The greatest changes in agricultural practices took place around 900AD. During this period, populations became more settled and farming became the predominant activity. The system of agriculture in use was the 'Open Field System', crops were grown in strips of land in a large field and animals were grazed on commons. Farming practices did not change significantly until the fourteenth century.

The craft of dry stone walling, as we know it today, owes much to the Scottish Drystane Dykers who probably mastered the art to blend in with the British farming system. Many of Britain's field walls were built between 1500 and 1900. The greatest time of construction would have been between 1760 and 1845 during the 'Enclosures Act'. The long walls stretching over the hills of upland Britain are our most recent – having been commissioned by the landowners and estates to mark the boundaries of the areas that they had claimed for themselves. Those walls forming very small enclosures, often found winding their way unevenly around homesteads, are some of the oldest and were built, it is thought, to retain animals of subsistence farming. Families farming the harsh uplands built many these before the Enclosures Act, but some were constructed during the Act in an attempt to claim the land for themselves. The larger landowners were more intent on acquiring more fertile, valuable areas of lowland Britain.

Although in lower areas the Enclosures Act led to the introduction of hedges and fences, in the wilder remote uplands it was difficult to establish other methods of marking boundaries. The abundant rocks and stones littering steep hillsides were utilized instead. Instead of following the contours of a hillside, the walls were erected from valley base to summit and beyond. Nowadays, to the untrained eye, they seem to be held in place by some incredibly strong invisible force.

The varied appearances and styles of this type of construction are down to the inherent differences in the availability and properties of the locally found stone.

The landscape of Great Britain is incredibly varied, often changing completely within a few miles. The reason for these dramatic transformations lies beneath the surface of the soil, in the large number of different types of bedrock. Individual rock types have varying properties, which leads to different patterns of erosion. This island has seen massive geological upheaval in the distant past, leading to rock types of different ages and constituents surfacing side by side despite being formed millions of years apart.

There are three divergent rock types: igneous, sedimentary and metamorphic. Igneous rocks are formed when hot molten rock cools down and solidifies. They appear in two forms, intrusive and extrusive. Intrusive rock cools below the surface and extrusive rock cools above ground. Granite is an example of an igneous rock. As igneous rocks tend to be crystalline, they are very hard and difficult to break and form areas of high ground. Whilst this property makes stone resistant to erosion, it has the disadvantage of leaving it very difficult to dress to shape using walling tools.

Sedimentary rock is formed when particles of material are laid down and subsequently compressed. The particles can arise as a result of erosion of pre-existing rock or from organic matter such as shells or bones from animals. There are many differing rocks of this type, but the two examples that are widely used by dry stone wallers are sandstone and limestone. Sandstone arises from compressed sand particles and shale, but originally derived from compressed mud. Limestone is made from the bodies of sea creatures and is predominantly calcium carbonate. Chalk is also predominantly calcium carbonate, but is a much softer rock than limestone.

Sedimentary rock is laid down in bedding planes and, as such, is easy to split along these planes. Whilst this leads to the rock being more resistant to erosion, it makes it ideal for the experienced dry stone wall builder to dress and use. Stone of this type tends to have good 'faces', which again makes it ideal for walling.

The third type of rock is metamorphic.

This rock is formed when existing rock (either sedimentary or igneous) is subjected to immense heat or pressure, or a combination of both. These conditions could have occurred at times when volcanic activity or earth movements were prevalent. Since most types of metamorphosed rock tend to be valuable, for instance marble, they are not likely to have been used for dry stone walling. However, one type of metamorphic rock is extremely common in Great Britain and that is slate. Slate was formed when shale was subjected to volcanic activity, and is prevalent in upland areas, particularly in Wales, Cornwall and parts of the Lake District. Slate is an easy-to-use stone for dry stone walling, hosting a number of useful properties including cleavage; this is where it is easy for a skilled person to break slate along the original bedding planes of the shale.

The natural lifespan and demise of a dry stone wall is dependent on erosion, and all three rock types are subject to this. Erosion is predominant in two forms, chemical and mechanical. Chemical erosion occurs when the actual constituents of the rock are dissolved by acid. This is called *chemical weathering*. Weathering takes place when carbon dioxide in the air combines with rainwater and falls to earth as acid rain. The damage is caused when the rain penetrates the stone. All rock types are susceptable to this action, however the harder rocks such as granite take millions of years to be eroded in this way. If acidic minerals are present the process can be speeded up. Limestone, chalk and slate have become more vulnerable since the advent of pollution.

Mechanical erosion occurs when natural variation in temperature causes the rock to expand and contract. This action results in large pieces breaking free from the main structure. The process is exacerbated when water penetrates along natural fault lines then freezes. Eventually this results in the formation of piles of boulders being formed in exposed rocky areas. This would have been one of the original sources of material for upland farmers to use for construction. Other sources included quarries, specifically excavated for enclosure purposes, and nearby river beds where walling stone was extracted.

Many of the contrasts in styles of walling throughout the British Isles arise from differences in the properties and availablity of local rock. As outlined earlier, there are many different bedrock types, all of which are millions of years old. An interesting thought for today's wallers, when they pick up a stone to add it to a new structure, is that the material could have been formed even before the dinosaurs roamed the Earth.

The oldest rocks are the Precambrian, which form some of the ancient sandstones of upland Wales and southern Scotland. The bedrock in these regions was formed 3,400 million years ago, before life began. Later volcanic activity pushed up mountain ranges and created igneous and metamorphic rocks; this included regions of granite in Dartmoor and the Lake District. The mountains in these regions are made of very hard rocks that have resisted erosion. Large slabs of granite were used to build a dry stone drovers bridge in Dartmoor; the structure is still in use today as a footbridge. At Grimspound, in Devon, there is a Bronze Age settlement that is completely surrounded by a dry stone wall made entirely of granite.

Following this period of upheaval, these islands became a desert. During this period the old red sandstones were formed. This excellent building stone is predominant in Devon (hence the name Devon Red sandstone), and forms a band up the west of Britain through the West Midlands, Shrewsbury, Chester and up to the north west of Cumbria. In the dark, peak area of the Peak District National Park a similar type of stone is present, known locally as Derbyshire Gritstone. In areas where this stone was present close to the surface, there are ample examples of ancient dry stone structures made from this distinctive material. Sandstone, no matter what form it presents itself, is easy to dress to size and shape – hence the beautiful, smooth faces usually associated with this style of wall.

During the Carboniferous period (between 345 million and 320 million years ago) Britain was covered with warm seas. Within this period limestone was formed by the compression of the remains of sea creatures. The presence of carboniferous limestone in this country has led to the formation of the distinctive landscapes of the Yorkshire Dales and the White Peak in the Peak District National Park. In these upland areas the construction of dry stone walls came into its own. The abundance of exposed areas of rock and availablity of piles of stone provided the ideal material for the hill farmers to construct stock-proof barriers. One of the great delights of walling with this type of limestone is the presence of fossils. If the waller is not careful, it is possible to spend more time painstakingly chipping away with the walling hammer to extract the specimens, than on the job in hand!

A different type of limestone was formed later, during the Jurassic period (around 195 million years ago). This limestone forms a ridge from Dorset through to the Cotswolds, and there is a second ridge which finishes in the North York Moors. In the Cotswolds there are many fine examples of dry stone walls constructed from this limestone. This type of limestone is harder than the carboniferous limestone, and is not so easy to wall with. The problem is mainly due to its small size and the lack of ideal stone to tie the walls together. It is for this reason that the Cotswolds walls are lower in height than any other region.

Chalk is a very soft rock and is present in Southern England, forming the bedrock of the North and South Downs. There is also an area of chalk in the east; this is the bedrock that resulted in the formation of the Yorkshire Wolds. Chalk contains bands of fossilized remains resulting in bands of darker flints. Although chalk has not been used extensively to form dry stone walls as stock barriers, ancient tribes used it to construct buildings. Some of these structures remain today, evidence of the durability of this construction method.

The newest type of rock in the British Isles was formed during a second period of volcanic activity as recently as one million years ago. During this time period the granites of the North of Scotland were formed. Dolerite was also formed in West Wales. This is the material used to build Stonehenge and there are examples of dry stone buildings made from this material in West Wales.

The origins of this rural craft are firmly rooted in the past, reaching back to a time before life as we know it began. The styles, shapes and appearances of dry stone walls are intertwined with the landscape and heritage of an area in a way that no other man-made structure ever can. The practitioner of this ancient art can be assured that, as he or she places each stone into a dry stone wall, the act entwines a piece of history into a natural landscape. A human touch in complete harmony with nature, enhancing the appearance and conservation value of the countryside. There are not many building techniques in use today that can boast these kinds of advantages!

CHAPTER 2

THE SECRETS WITHIN A DRY STONE WALL

Many of us, at some stage, have looked upon these ancient structures, wondering how they have managed to survive the onslaught of the years. With no cement to keep them together, why don't they fall down? Like most things in life, however, nothing withstands the passing of time without some element of decay. Theft, livestock pushing against well-built layers, people taking short cuts across fields, climbing walls and dislodging top stones, can all lead to a wall's demise. Urban sprawl has played its part also, as has the unfortunate demise of the farming community. Thankfully, within our national parks and conservation areas a programme of preservation is in place and there are plenty of opportunities for anyone wishing to take up the craft.

To many people dry stone walling is an enigma, to some it is a matter of simple technique. A fascinating technique that, through the chapters of this book, will hopefully become clear.

The flexibility of dry stone wall construction is such that any stone, whether it be sandstone, limestone, slate or granite, can be pieced together to form an effective, long-lasting garden feature or field boundary. Although walling styles can vary up and down the country, the basic building principles remain the same throughout.

Like a common, mortared brick wall a dry stone wall has a foundation, an intermediate section and a row of top stones, often called *coping-stones*. Each stone, where possible, crosses the joins of the ones below. This is where the similarity ends. Unlike a mortared wall, where sand and cement are the main ingredient for keeping the structure together, a dry stone wall relies solely on differing sizes of stone, correctly placed, to prevent it from falling down.

There are two main types of dry stone wall: a retaining wall and the common, double-skinned wall you see enclosing our fields and meadows. Retaining walls are designed to minimize the effect of erosion by creating a hard barrier between the open air and land, thus preventing steep slopes from collapsing. They are often seen keeping soil from falling on to footpaths and roadways. It is this style of wall that will be of more interest to the enthusiastic gardener because they are ideal for creating planting beds and aesthetic backdrops for ponds. A double-skinned wall can be described as a self-supporting structure used to partition fields and gardens.

So, how do these fragile looking structures remain sturdy and aloft when all that is keeping them together are the random shaped stones of the natural terrain?

The standard dimensions of a dry stone wall are approximately: 4ft 6in (1.4m) in height, 2ft 3in (76cm) at foundation width and 14in (35cm) in width at the top. The wall is comprised of two sides or *skins*, which face out, and is built in a succession of interlocked *layers* or *courses*. Large *foundation stones* help to provide a secure base for the rest of the outer stones, called *face-stones*, which are gradually laid in single courses to form a wall. Unlike double-skinned mortared walls that are built vertically, a dry stone wall is erected in the form of an apex. This is called the *slope* or *batter*. The batter helps to disperse the wall's weight evenly toward the ground, ensuring that any movement, natural or otherwise, is forced in this direction rather than outward or towards the centre. The batter is achieved by using a set of devices called *batter-frames*. These are comprised of two wooden structures that represent the width and height of the desired dry stone wall under construction. They are secured at each end of the wall, connected to one another by *string-lines*. The string-lines represent the wall's outer faces and are used as a template when laying face-stones. The use of the batter-frame and string-lines enables the waller to erect a wall free of bulges and serious irregularities. This is achieved by making sure that the front of a face-stone is laid in parallel alignment with the string.

As each stone is placed on the wall, it is strengthened from behind with pieces of rubble called *wedges*, *pinning* or *pinning-stones*. These are small wedged-shaped pieces of stone, pushed under the gaps at the back of each face-stone to secure them to the wall. Random stone is unstable, even placed on a flat surface it will wobble. Strategically placed pinning will stop any movement like this from happening.

As the stones are laid and *pinned*, gaps appear in the wall's centre or *heart*. These holes are filled with more rubble, called *hearting-stone*. Whenever possible, face-stones are placed with their entire length into the wall, resting on the hearting. This helps to tie the face-stones to the centre of the wall. *Through-stones* or *throughs* are used every 3–4ft (90–120cm) to bind both sides of the wall together. The method of using throughs is to place them on a single course, halfway up the wall. This is called the *through-band*. The top layer of wall is called the *coping*. *Coping-stones* bridge the two skins of wall and are tightly locked together to form a rigid course. The top courses of face-stones are built with smaller material, the use of coping ensures that these thinner, weaker courses are securely tied together. A wall without coping is a prime candidate for decay. The heart of the wall will be susceptible to weather erosion and its supporting face-stones easily pushed off by livestock or people.

Just as the top of a wall is sealed by the coping-stones, the end of the wall has to be secured also. This is accomplished by building *wall-ends* or *cheek-ends*. These sections are incorporated into each course as the wall gains in height. Like through-stones, *end-stones* should be long enough to span the width of any given course and are laid utilizing a two-on-one or one-on-two technique. 'One' is a through stone placed across the wall's width. 'Two' are similar-sized stones, called *runners*, which literally run down the line of each of the wall's two skins. A further through-stone is laid on the runners and so it continues until the wall reaches the desired height, and is ready for the layer of coping-stones.

When bricks are cemented together they become one rigid object. Movement in a rigid, brick wall can create serious, structural faults. This may result in the majority of the feature having to be rebuilt. Every stone in a dry wall – including hearting and pinning – is an independent object, yet they all serve one purpose, to stop the wall from falling down. The dry stone wall, to some degree, is flexible and any future movement ensures that the structure falls together as opposed to apart. The finished wall, if built correctly, can settle as much as 6in (15cm) within its first year.

Variations on Style

Although the basic principles of building dry stone walls are the same regardless of the style, there are some structural mutations that are put together in an entirely different way. These styles are discussed in the later chapters. For the most part this book pays attention to the fundamentals of the craft. Once the aspiring wall builder has grasped these principles, the subtle changes will be easy to adjust to. A useful metaphor is knowing how to drive a small car then climbing into a large four-wheel-drive and being relieved that at least the foot pedals and steering wheel are in the same place, even though you have to adjust to the different gear systems.

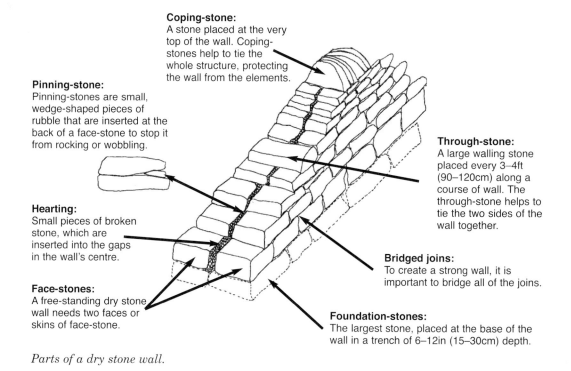

Coping-stone:
A stone placed at the very top of the wall. Coping-stones help to tie the whole structure, protecting the wall from the elements.

Pinning-stone:
Pinning-stones are small, wedge-shaped pieces of rubble that are inserted at the back of a face-stone to stop it from rocking or wobbling.

Hearting:
Small pieces of broken stone, which are inserted into the gaps in the wall's centre.

Face-stones:
A free-standing dry stone wall needs two faces or skins of face-stone.

Through-stone:
A large walling stone placed every 3–4ft (90–120cm) along a course of wall. The through-stone helps to tie the two sides of the wall together.

Bridged joins:
To create a strong wall, it is important to bridge all of the joins.

Foundation-stones:
The largest stone, placed at the base of the wall in a trench of 6–12in (15–30cm) depth.

Parts of a dry stone wall.

CHAPTER 3

GETTING STARTED

Getting Hold of Stone

Whether building gaps or starting from scratch, a source of material will be needed. A collapsed section of wall may appear to have an abundance of stone littered here and there around its base, but don't take it for granted that there will be enough to rebuild the section. Work on the principle that this section of wall would have contained just the right amount of stone to complete the original job. Whatever the cause of the damage, the resulting fall may have broken coping, split an important through-stone and crushed a quantity of face-stones. You can count on the fact that a good number of the original pinning and hearting-stones are scattered or buried somewhere under the soil. If you are lucky, you will be able to dig the majority of this out. Quite often the only way to replace the pinning and hearting is to either have a new supply or break some of the existing face-stones with a hammer. In the long run, this will prove unproductive, as it will have the effect of diminishing the supply of face-stones. Taking theft in to account, be prepared to import an extra 25–30 per cent of material.

The type of available stone largely depends on where you live. Also it is well to remember that if you reside in a National Park, an Area of Outstanding Natural Beauty (AONB) or a local Conservation Area you will have to use whatever material is in keeping with the locality. Advice on these matters can be obtained from the local planning authority. Quarries situated near areas where dry stone walls feature abundantly in the landscape usually cater for the walling community. Before contacting the quarry manager it is necessary to work out the quantities you will need – around 1 ton per metre of wall built to a height of 4ft 6in (1.4m). This will be enough to provide for pinning, hearting, throughs, face-stones, end-stones and coping. The cost (in 2001) varies from as little as £30 per ton to as much as £120 per ton depending on the type of stone required. This does not include VAT. Even if only a small quantity of stone is required, unless you have access to a suitable towing vehicle, there will be a delivery charge added to the cost. Stone purchased from quarries is often called *random walling*.

Another good source is the local papers. In the classified section there are often adverts from individuals offering 'rockery stone' for sale. Sometimes it is possible to pick up a bargain, but it is worth checking the local market price before striking a deal or you may end up paying an extortionate cost. Theft of stone is very common, so it is advisable to make sure the material you are about to

Quarries provide a source of walling stone – Berwyn Slate Quarry Llangollen.

purchase is from a legitimate source. On occasions, within the private adverts, I have found a person only too willing for the stone to be taken off their hands for nothing. It does come at price though. You will have to arrange collection and delivery yourself. If the project requires more than one ton it could mean a hefty fuel bill and the possible purchase or hire of a pickup or double-axle trailer.

As regards stone, the majority of builders' merchants deal only in pre-cast bricks and aggregates. Garden centres concentrate mainly on ornamental stone features, but a clued up assistant or manager could point you in the right direction. You could even try popping down to the local Farmers Union office or DIY outlet and glance over the private adver-

tising boards. There is stone available, but you may have to make a determined effort to locate a good supply.

Safety

Like all manual tasks that involve the lifting or carrying of large construction materials and the use of working tools, safety is of paramount importance. If repairing a damaged wall, it is important to have respect for the possibility of collapse at an unexpected moment. The section of wall you wish to repair could be tottering on the edge of disaster merely awaiting for someone to remove a vital supporting stone permitting it to finally crash to the ground. Consider also the fact that most dry stone walls were built upon rugged and uneven land. There is always a risk of stumbling or tripping over a pile of stone.

Common walling injuries include broken feet and toes, broken or bruised hands and fingers, eye injury and back strain. Other problems to be aware of, especially when walling in remote places are exhaustion, hunger and heat stroke. Nature throws many things at us, including the threat of hypothermia in the height of summer. If you are going to have to work in open country it is important to take along the correct equipment (*see below*), and not to forget appropriate provision for sustenance. A good packed lunch and a flask of hot drink (perhaps a cold drink in summer) are essential.

The following is a list of items that should be used when working in the open on a dry stone wall:

- steel toe-capped boots or wellingtons;
- strong safety gloves (try to avoid the rubber variety, as most natural stone is abrasive and will shred them to ribbons in no time at all);
- eye protectors;
- first-aid kit.

In upland regions the weather can change drastically and it is a good idea to have some waterproofs and an extra fleece or sweater. Also, in summer remember to cover up with lightweight clothing and use a sunscreen. A hat is a good idea in both summer and winter.

The wider availability of mobile phones has revolutionized safety within the rural environment. There are some places, however, where signals are either weak or non-existent. As a precaution, leave your position and grid reference with someone you trust, including the estimated time you will be finished at the end of the day.

Dry stone walling involves the lifting and manipulation of uneven, heavy objects. It is advisable to learn a good lifting technique and never be too proud to ask for a hand with the heavier stones.

Danger lurks around many corners, not least with the building material. Slate and limestone, for example, can be razor sharp, sandstone is very abrasive to the hands and fingers, and all stone, when hit with a hammer, has the tendency to produce shards of sharp stone that can fly toward unprotected eyes.

If the project requires the dismantling of an old section of wall, survey the area for likely hazards. The stone could be unstable and about to collapse at any moment. Carefully follow the guidance given later in the book to ensure that you do not place yourself in danger of falling stones. Debris such as broken glass, pottery and rusty nails are often found in the centre of old walls; all these artefacts can lead to an injury of some sort.

Wasps sometimes build their nests within recesses of old walls, so look for signs of the insect's activity along the portion to be rebuilt. The wasp grubs within the nest are a handy source of bait for anglers. If you don't fancy dealing with it yourself, maybe a local fisherman will take the nest off your hands. If you know you are allergic to their stings then you should probably leave them well alone. The local authority will have a department that can deal with this problem, and sometimes do not charge if the nest is alongside a public footpath. A reputable pest control company may also be able to help.

To conclude, pay great attention to personal safety, but also be aware of others in the area. Make sure that there is good communication between all parties, and ensure that warnings are given before carrying out any act that may pose a risk to others working with you or passing by.

Tools of the Trade

As with all ancient crafts the most important tools you will need are your hands and a level head. I have quite often built up a gap in a farmer's field with no less than a pair of gloves and a hammer. A selection of tools will make the job of

walling much easier and a list of the most useful items is given below. Specialist tools are quite expensive and unless you are planning to do a lot of walling, you might not think the investment worthwhile. For that reason I have listed some alternatives that may be found hanging up in the average garden shed.

Walling hammer. This tool is similar to a lump hammer and is designed for breaking and dressing stone. Walling hammers come in differing sizes and weights, but they all have a blunt end for breaking stone and a chisel end for cutting and shaping.

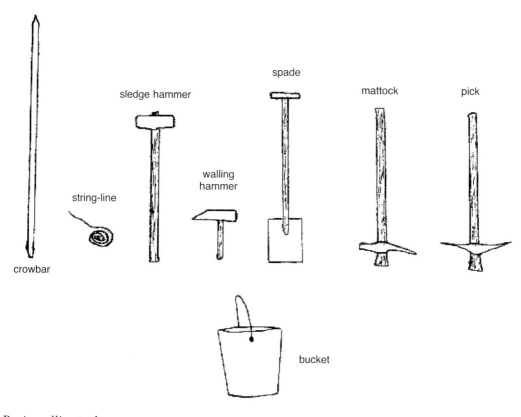

Basic walling tools.

Lump hammer. Can be used instead of a walling hammer.

Sledge hammer. Used for breaking big stones.

Spade. For digging out foundations and clearing debris.

Mattock or pick. Mattocks and picks are ideal for breaking up small tree roots and loosening hard ground.

Crowbar. A crowbar is shaped like a spear and made out of strong metal. One end of the bar is pointed and is therefore ideal for breaking up compacted ground. The other end of the bar is chisel shaped and mainly used for splitting awkward stone within a foundation trench. A crowbar can also be used as a lever to move large pieces of rock around a work site.

Rake. To help tidy up the work site at the end of the day.

Bucket. Handy for collecting hearting stone.

Wheelbarrow. For moving quantities of stone and soil around the walling area.

Nylon string-line. Used in conjunction with the batter-frame as a guide to making the wall's face as smooth as possible.

Line level. A line level is a small spirit level, designed to hang on a string. Setting up the string-lines with this inexpensive tool allows for very accurate placing of face-stones. This results in a highly aesthetic finished product.

Batter-frame. A wooden frame, which if used correctly, helps the dry stone waller to build the wall to the required slope. On some jobs, where wooden frames could hinder the walling process, metal rods can be used instead.

Checking your Tools

Before using any tool, it is important to check that it is in good order and suitable for the job in hand. A loose hammerhead may slip off the shaft causing injury to oneself or another. Loose-fitting pick and mattock heads have the tendency to slide down the shaft, causing potential injury to the user. If the shafts are rotten, replace them. If they have shrunk, which is sometimes the case, a long soak in a bucket of water will help to swell the wood to the metal.

Working with Walling Tools

- Don't swing mattocks, picks, sledge hammers and walling hammers above head height. This could unbalance the user when working on a hillside or cause injury to someone behind.
- Warn others before using tools to break stone.
- It is a good idea not to leave unused tools standing upright in case someone walks into them. Push the prongs of rakes into the ground. Find a safe storage area away from any paths and use it all the time. This way you will know where the tools are and won't be wasting time searching for them, and you won't inadvertently trip over them.
- Wear some form of eye protection when breaking stone.

Making a Batter-Frame

Batter-frames come in two equal parts for placing at either end of the proposed wall. It is appropriate to make sure they are the same height and width of the wall. Each frame is placed at either end of the proposed wall, and joined together with strings. The strings represent the wall's face-stones. As each course is completed the string lines are moved higher to accommodate the next course of stones.

The importance of the dry stone wall's batter can not be stressed enough. The wall's stability relies on it and without it the finished article could turn out to be an ugly, uneven, mass. There are times, of course, where the use of batter-frames could encumber the walling process. Jobs such as rebuilding a gap within a small section of wall or constructing a stone step-over stile (explained later on in the book), can be built using string-lines and pins attached to the two good ends of the wall under repair. Batter-frames are only needed when a new wall section, which includes one or two wall-ends, is created or rebuilt.

Making a batter-frame is a very simple, inexpensive affair and all it requires is a fundamental understanding of woodwork, a small amount of wooden baton and a few basic tools and fittings. The following is a list of materials and fittings, which is enough to build the two units that make up a batter-frame:

- 31ft (9.5m) of 2in by 1in (5cm by 2.5cm) timber batons;
- 20 × 1.5in (4cm) wood screws (or nails);
- hand saw;
- screwdriver;
- electric or hand drill;
- tape measure or ruler;
- set square;
- pencil.

Working on a secure table or workbench, measure the correct sizes of timber required and carefully saw it to the following sizes:

- 4 × 54in (1.4m) lengths (for the main batter sides 'A' and 'B' – see diagram on facing page);
- 2 × 14in (36cm) lengths (for the top batons 'C');
- 2 × 27in (68cm) lengths (for bottom batons 'D');
- 2 × 36in (90cm) lengths (for the two braces 'E').

Refer to the diagram. With the all the pieces of sawn timber in place, find the centres of batons C and D and mark them using a set square and pencil. Without disturbing baton C, move baton D down the frame, leaving a 36in (90cm) gap between the two.

From the centre line of baton C, measure 7in (18cm) either side of the line. Again, mark with a set square and pencil. The measurement between the two outer lines should not exceed 14in (36cm). Repeat the same for baton D.

Still working with baton D, now measure 13in (33cm) either side of the centre line (this is a second set of measurements for this baton). Mark a line with a set square and pencil. The measurement between the outer lines should not exceed 26in (66cm).

Take batter sides A and B and place them on top of batons C and D, lining them up with the 7in (18cm) markers on both batons, thus forming a rectangle.

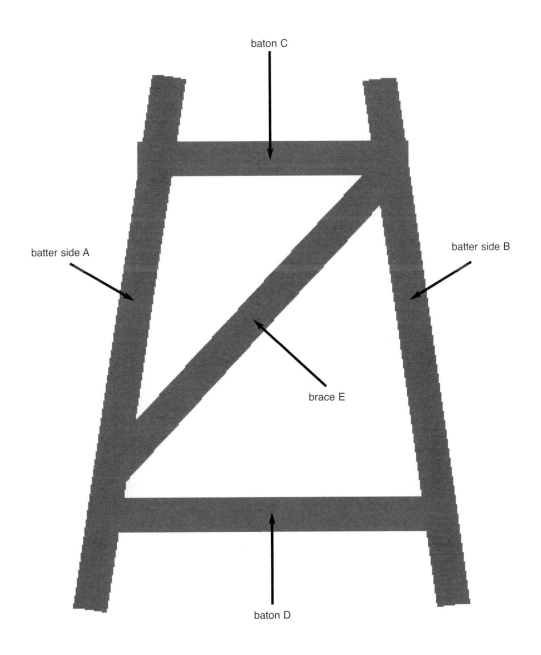

Parts of the batter-frame.

Finding the centre of baton C and D.

Measuring the diagonals.

Moving batter sides to the 13in (33cm) mark.

Fixing the frame together.

Attaching brace E.

Measure the diagonal from the corner of A and C to the corner of D and B. Do the same for the opposite diagonal. If both measurements are equal, the frame, at this stage, is true and square.

Working with batter sides A and B, move the bottom ends along baton D until their outer edges reach the 13in (33cm) markers on either side.

Make sure the tops of A and B remain aligned with the 7in (18cm) markers on baton C. During this operation, it is very important that batons C and D are not moved, and the distance of 36in (90cm) between them is maintained. The frame will now be set up to the required batter.

Holding the frame securely in place, drill a pilot hole in all four corners, countersink and screw the frame together. If a hammer and nails are to be used, great care must be taken to ensure the frame remains within the markers. If in doubt, keep checking the measurements.

Before the frame is ready to use, a diagonal brace (E) must be attached to ensure that the batter does not become misaligned during the walling procedure.

To finish the frame, trim C, D, and E flush with the outside edges of batter rails A and B.

Build the second frame using the same method.

The completed frame.

CHAPTER 4

BASIC WALLING TECHNIQUE

The primary role of a dry stone wall is stock enclosure. As most upland areas in Britain are used for grazing sheep and sometimes cattle, these boundaries have to be an adequate barrier. Most breeds of sheep will find it difficult to climb or jump a near vertical face of 4ft 6in (1.4m) and this is why the majority of walls are constructed to this height. Within a few regions of Britain this basic dimension can vary due to the size and quality of local stone. In the Cotswolds, for example, the individual portions of limestone are too small to create an effective 4ft 6in barrier resulting in most walls there only reaching 3ft 3in (1m) in height.

As a general rule of thumb, the depth of the wall is dependent on its finished height. The width at the base should be half the height and the width at the top should be half the width of the bottom. This will mean that a wall of 4ft 6in (1.4m) in height will be 2ft 3in (68cm) wide at foundation level and around 14in (36cm) in width where the coping should go.

The Golden Rules of Dry Stone Walling

At different points in the book it will be apparent that certain elements of the craft are described repeatedly. No matter how diverse the style of wall is, its construction will follow a set of basic procedures that are second nature to a skilled waller.

Fundamental and important techniques, if employed successfully, will ensure the finished wall is a stable structure. It is hoped that when you have finished reading this book they will be firmly imprinted on your mind. I have called them the Golden Rules.

Before Construction

- Separate large stones for use as foundations, throughs and end-stones.
- Separate stone that will be ideal for the coping.
- Organize the supply of stone into size-ordered rows or piles.

Building the Wall

- Keep a safe working distance between the unused stone and the wall under construction.
- Use the larger stones for the bottom courses, gradually using them in order of decreasing size when the wall is built higher.
- Every stone, where possible, should be placed with its length towards the centre of the wall. Stone set the other way could pivot out when the wall settles.
- The stone should either sit on the course horizontally or with its back slightly raised. This will deflect any rainwater from the important heart of the wall. To aid drainage even further, try to find a face of the stone that will slope away from the wall.
- Insert pinners under each stone when it is placed on the wall. Use as much pinning-stone as required until the stone in question sits firm. Avoid inserting pinners from the outer face of the wall as they may fall away when the finished wall settles, or small animals could dislodge them.
- Most styles of walling require their centres to be filled with hearting-stone. Unless the method of walling calls for a soil/rubble mixture, always use pieces of broken stone. When filling the wall with hearting it is important to be careful not to disturb the pinners under the face stones.
- Always build one course of wall before starting on the next. On some projects this is not possible, and it may be necessary to build a small section of wall to coping height. Use this method if it is a repair of an existing structure that

cannot be finished in one day and stock proofing is essential. If you have to do this the courses of the wall should be left stepped, ready to tie in the rest of the wall.
- Cross the joins of each stone on every course. Never allow a join to run-on more than two courses high, but try to avoid this if possible.
- Never drop a stone onto a wall, it will unsettle the courses below or crush your fingers. Lay the stone gently on top of another and enlist the help of another person if it is too heavy to do this.
- When dismantling a wall, always lift the stone vertically from the course. Dragging stone may cause a major collapse of the lower sections.
- Take the wall down course by course.

Evaluating Walling Material

If a quarry has delivered the stone, the waller will be faced with a disorganized pile of bedrock. For the job in hand to go smoothly and without frustration, it is better to grade the stone in piles according to size, on either side of the proposed wall. This can be done in one of two ways. Firstly, make piles of stone in the order of the size they are going to be laid into the wall. Find the longest and heaviest stones for the foundations and place them within a safe working distance, close to the walling site. The next pile to be created should include the stones for the first 3–4 courses above the foundation. Ideally these will be fairly large chunks, but light enough to manipulated into place by one

This is a well-built wall. The joins have been bridged and the large stones have been used for the foundations.

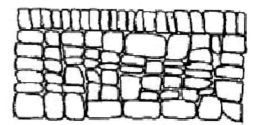

A weak wall. Too many running joins and some large stones have been laid on the top of the wall.

The correct way to insert pinning-stones is from behind.

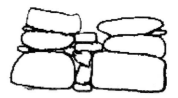

Pinning-stones pushed in the front will fall out and weaken the wall.

The correct way to lay face-stones. Horizontal or slightly sloping away from the wall.

The two skins of the wall will not bind together if the face-stones are laid like this.

Good practice and bad practice.

person. A third pile would ideally contain smaller face-stones for the upper courses. Create one last pile with the left-over rubble for use as hearting and pinning. Once construction is under way, it will be astonishing how rapidly the pile of hearting will disappear. With this in mind, the worst looking walling stone, that is material that has no smooth faces and is completely rounded, can be separated from other stone and broken up if necessary.

The most important stones to look for at this stage are the ones for the coping, throughs and wall-ends. During the construction phase it is very tempting to use them prematurely, laying them on a course when a normal face-stone would be sufficient. Store these stones away from the main bulk of materials. There is nothing more frustrating than discovering that there is no stone available to create a through-band or running out of coping-stones two or three feet from the end of a project. Further more, it is infuriating to realize that these missing items have been diligently placed and pinned somewhere on the middle courses.

An alternative method of grading stone is to sort them in size-ordered rows (either side of the wall again). It is time consuming, but time spent now will greatly reduce the time it takes when looking for a stone to fit an awkward gap.

Grading the stone.

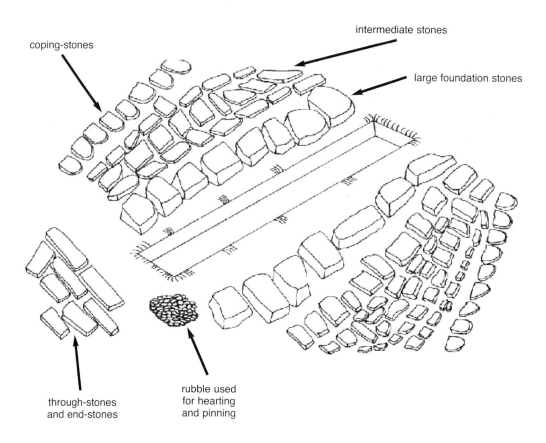

coping-stones

intermediate stones

large foundation stones

through-stones
and end-stones

rubble used
for hearting
and pinning

Grading stone.

Laying the Foundations

The foundation is probably the most important segment of any building, dry stone walls being no exception. Considering that one metre of wall can contain at least one ton of stone, whatever is responsible for keeping it up in the years to come will have to be reliable and strong. No matter how well the face-stones are laid, if the foundations are weak it will eventually collapse upon itself. A firm foundation course is created by using large stones that require little or no pinning, sitting in a trench of suitable depth with a stable subsoil or bedrock base. If the foundation stones are such that they require pinning, these pinners will be pushed further into the ground as the wall settles, forcing the centre of the wall downward. This in turn will produce a shift in material on the upper courses, dislodging additional pinning and hearting until the wall eventually gives way.

An obvious recipe for disaster is a foundation course resting on the surface of the soil. Stones will be pushed into the ground causing uneven settling or the weight of the wall could cause the entire course to slide if the area is prone to a high water table. A properly excavated foundation trench, with vertical sides, will prevent this type of damage.

Excavating a correct foundation trench is vitally important and can involve many hours of backbreaking work, particularly if the ground is rocky or laden with compacted debris. Any tussocks of grass or hard-stemmed plants such as dock or nettle on the proposed line of the wall must be removed, along with their root systems. If they are allowed to grow back through the finished wall, they could dislodge hearting-stones and pinning.

To begin the trench, measure and mark out the area to be excavated. If there are existing walls in the vicinity take advantage of their width dimensions and use

them as a guide for the new wall, that way the new wall will blend in with its surroundings. If there aren't any other walls, refer to the dimensions described at the beginning of this chapter. Starting at one of the proposed wall-ends, use a tape measure to determine accurately the intended width of the foundation trench and then insert a stake into the ground at each of the two points marking the corners of the wall-end. A lump hammer or walling hammer can be used to knock them in if the ground is too hard. Repeat this procedure for the other end of the wall.

To create a digging template, tie string-lines to the two stakes at one of the ends then run them out, just above ground

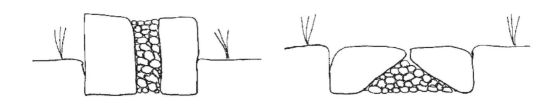

These foundation stones are unstable because they are sitting on their narrow sides.

In this diagram the full weight of the wall is resting on the hearting.

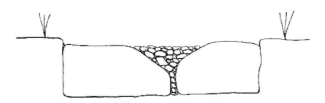

This is a solid foundation. The widest and flattest sides of the stone are sitting on the ground, firmly in the trench.

Good practice and bad practice (foundation).

Measuring the foundation trench.

Cutting the sides of the trench with a spade, following the string-line.

Excavating the trench.

level, to the stakes at the other end. Pulling them tight, tie the strings onto these stakes, making sure that both lines are running parallel and there is an equal width between them down the entire length of the proposed trench.

With a spade, work down the outside of the strings pushing it vertically into the ground as far as it will go until the foundation's length and width have been clearly marked.

Before shovelling out it is advisable to find a suitable place for the waste matter, otherwise, if left dumped around the work site, it will be trampled on making it difficult to clear away when the job is complete or, if it rains, it will become a dangerous quagmire. Soil can be dumped

onto a compost heap or around shrubs and trees. On no account use the soil for filling the wall's centre unless the style requires it.

Working along the inside of the lines, excavate the trench, keeping the edges vertical, until firm subsoil or bedrock is reached. This can be anything from 6in (15cm) to a maximum 12in (30cm) depending on the region. Any stone uncovered at this point is a bonus and can be added to the relevant walling piles or rows.

Having excavated the foundation, flatten the base as much as possible by walking up and down the trench, eliminating any slopes and undulations that can seriously undermine the wall. Remove any

Constructing the wall-end, showing the one through-stone on two runners.

protruding stone that may cause the foundation to become unstable. Ramming in small stones with a sledge hammer or tamper until the ground becomes hard can firm soft spots up.

The trench is now ready to hold the foundations. The first stones to be laid will be the ones for both wall-ends. These can either be throughs (stones that span the entire width of the trench) or runners (stones laid on each side of the trench, following the line of the wall).

Once the wall-ends are set the rest of the foundation course can be manoeuvred into place. Some of these stones can be very heavy and may require two persons to lift them in. Before handling a stone it is a good idea to ascertain how it will sit once it is in place. This will avoid major adjustments that could crush the trench sides or gouge out the base. Find the largest and flattest surface of the stone and manipulate to fit before moving it in.

Whenever possible, lay the stones with their lengths protruding into the centre, but avoid the situation where one cannot be placed on the other side. If this happens either source a shorter stone or lay the existing one down the length of the trench as a last resort. The best foundations are laid below the depths of the top-soil, but any tall stone that is going to loom above the trench is better placed here rather than further up the wall. As

Great care should be taken when manoeuvring heavy foundation stones into the trench.

Checking that the foundation stones are secure.

soon as a stone is put in place a series of fine adjustments can be carried out to make sure it is butted up tightly to its neighbour and is running parallel with the sides of the trench.

When the last foundation stone is securely set, fill the centre of the whole course with large pieces of hearting, taking time to fill all the nooks and crannies under each stone. Keep the tops of the stones clear by only filling the wall to the height of the lowest stones on the course. Test the foundations by applying downward pressure with both hands, gently rocking the stones from side to side and backwards and forwards. Light pressure with the feet can be applied also, but avoid walking on the course and only use this method for the foundations, not the other courses of wall. If any stone shows signs of excessive movement, it will need resetting. If the foundation proves to be secure, all that remains to complete this course is to remove the string-lines and stakes.

The sheer nature of random stone is such that it is likely that the majority of stones will differ in height, and some will protrude above the trench. As long as they are resting firmly in the confines of the trench and can be easily built on, a strong foundation for the rest of the wall will have been achieved.

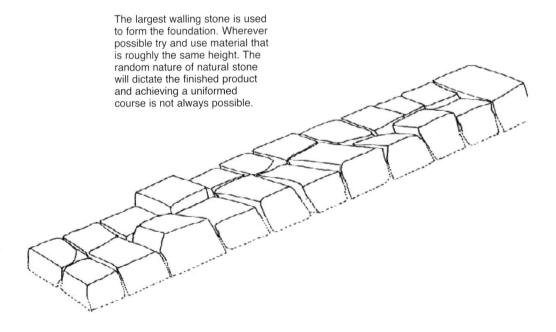

The largest walling stone is used to form the foundation. Wherever possible try and use material that is roughly the same height. The random nature of natural stone will dictate the finished product and achieving a uniformed course is not always possible.

When working at the wall-ends it is advisable to choose stone of a similar height. This will form a stable base for the end-stone on the next course.

Completed foundation.

Setting up the Batter-Frames

There are number of ways to set up the batter-frames. Securing them to two stakes at either end of the wall is one option, but this may not work on bedrock. Adding a prop at the back of each frame is another. The most common method is to attach guidelines to the top of the frames and fasten them to the ground with wooden or metal pegs. Some wallers prefer to use metal rods. They are less cumbersome and can be inserted into the ground. The way the frames are set up is ultimately a matter of personal preference. The important issue here is to produce the right batter for the wall.

Having successfully secured the frames, attach the string-lines for the face-stones. The lines should be tied to the frames at both ends of the wall and no more than 5in (12cm) above the lowest foundation-stone. They must be tensioned to reduce any slack and the width between them, as they run parallel down either side of the wall, should be equal.

Preparing the Waller to Lay the Face-Stones

To the uninitiated, building a dry stone wall using just random stone can appear daunting, and to place one on top of

Guidelines attached
to both frames are
secured to the
ground with wooden
stakes or metal pins.

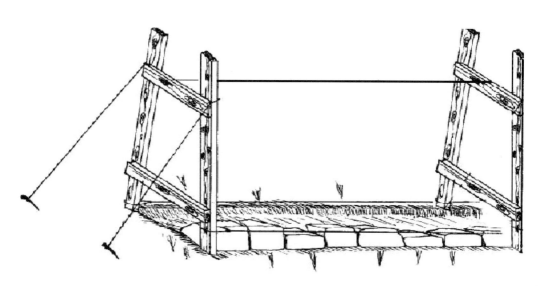

Securing the batter-frame.

another to form a long-lasting, solid structure, virtually impossible. The most important ingredient to the craft is the understanding of what to look for in the stone and knowing where and how to lay it on the wall. This is not some mysterious technique that only the walling community is able to comprehend, but more of a state of mind that comes with hands-on experience. Some people can grasp it straight away, after the first few courses of face-stone. For others it can take a little bit longer, but not as long as learning to drive, for instance.

When searching for face-stone the experienced dry stone waller automatically asks him- or herself a number of important questions, but not necessarily in the same order as below.

1. Does it have a vertical side that can face out from the wall? Believe it or not almost all random stone has an aesthetic edge, which can face out from the wall. Ideally the waller looks for a face that is slightly angled away from the wall. This helps to deflect rainwater from the centre.

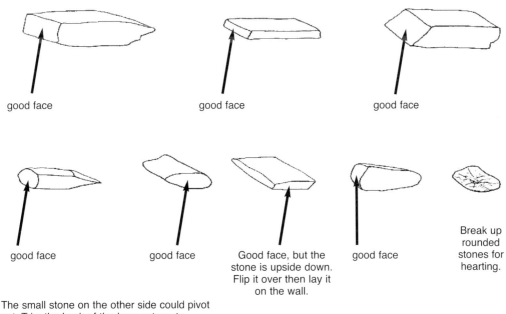

good face

good face

good face

good face

good face

Good face, but the stone is upside down. Flip it over then lay it on the wall.

good face

Break up rounded stones for hearting.

The small stone on the other side could pivot out. Trim the back of the larger stone to create more room on the course.

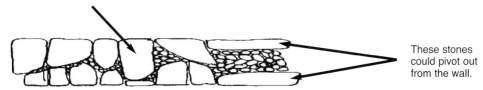

These stones could pivot out from the wall.

Using the right face of the stone.

2. Can the next course be built on top of it? If the top of the stone is too angular with hardly any flat surface area, then there is a possibility that the stone above will move, even when the wall is complete.

3. Will it leave enough room for the stone that is going to be laid on the other side of the wall? If the face-stone is laid, but only leaves just one or two inches of room for the stone on the neighbouring side, then this part of the wall could become unstable when the wall settles. This is called *walling out*.

The face-stones create the wall's batter and aesthetic appearance and it is vitally important that each one is laid following the basic principles. Any mistakes made now may not become apparent until after the wall settles, by then it will be too late to rectify them. Dry stone walls are not just built using strength and physical activity; the process requires an immense amount of concentration and mental thought processes. If at any time during construction concentration wanes, and you become totally bogged down and unable to select the right stone, do not panic! It happens to the best and most experienced. The only way to get around this problem is to take a break and think about something completely different. Upon returning to the task the answer is invariably there waiting.

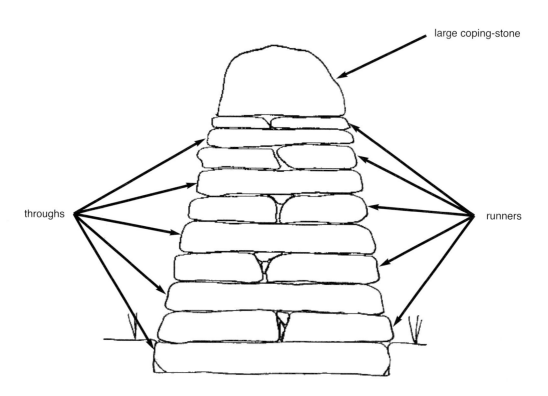

large coping-stone

throughs

runners

Parts of a wall-end.

Laying Stones for the Wall-Ends

The first face-stones to be laid on any new course of wall should be the ones for both the wall-ends. This method ensures that the end-stones, which need to be firm and long, are laid on to the course utilizing as much room as required. If a wall-end were to be laid last, then the face-stone on the course may impede a through or runner.

Wall-ends are best described as independently constructed pillars, acting like bookends or stoppers for the rest of the face-stones, pinning and hearting. They should be built at the start and finish of every dry stone wall or when there is break for a gateway or footpath access. Their primary role is to protect the wall from damage by livestock, people and the weather. It is for this reason that the stones should be smooth and large, enabling them to be placed without having to be pinned.

There is actually no rule as to whether or not the first end-stones in the foundation trench ought to be throughs or runners, but always use the largest stones available.

Once the first stones are in place, finish the course of wall by building the first two skins of face-stones between them, bringing their height as level as possible with the tops of the end-stones. Depending on the initial stones, start the

Random stone produces an uneven top to the course.

Levelling the uneven surface with smaller stones.

Wall-end showing arrangement of runners and throughs. (Wall built by students at Walford College.)

next course by using either throughs or runners (if throughs were used on the foundation then use runners on the first course or vice versa). Again, build up the two skins of face-stone in between. Repeat this procedure, alternating throughs and runners at the wall-ends, until the course is finished.

There are some important points to bear in mind during this procedure. Keep the wall-ends vertical at all times, checking them with a spirit level as the courses go on. Take care not to use small hearting stones between runners as they will fall out the end of the wall. On occasion the width of the runners may not be ideal for the base of the wall, leaving too wide a gap. If there is no large stone available, use three or four runners instead of two.

Laying the Face-Stones for the Lower Courses

It is easier to lay stone when one is looking directly at the wall. Large face-stones can be placed on the course without having to drag them over one skin to the other, which will unsettle the face-stones already in position. Always work from one wall-end to the next, building both skins at the same time before starting on the course above.

On these courses it is easy to lay a row of face-stones on one side of the wall then cross over to work on the opposite skin. As the wall is built higher, this action becomes increasingly difficult. Experienced craftsmen have mastered the technique of building two skins from one side.

Inserting pinning-stone.

For a novice this is not recommended until sufficient experience is attained in laying the face-stone accurately. If there is an existing access point, like a stile or gate, it will not be too difficult to work from alternate sides. If access is restricted, the only alternative is to carefully scale the wall, resetting any stone disturbed during the process.

For the first course of face-stone, look for the largest stones available and place them carefully on top of the foundations, abutting the sides of each one together and bridging the joins of the course below. When a stone sits on the wall the back of it should be 1/10in (0.5mm) higher than the face to aid water run off. Stones that tilt towards the centre will be pushed down even further as the wall settles. Once in position, manipulate the face-stone until the front is parallel with the string-line. Test the stone for stability by applying downward pressure on the front with one hand and rocking it from side to side and backward and forwards. If this test produces movement it will require pinning-stones to firm it up. Insert these from behind with the other hand whilst still employing the same downward pressure until the stone is secure.

Before inserting a pinning-stone, apply downward pressure to the front of the face-stone with your hand. With pressure still applied on the stone, insert the pinner(s) at the back with the other hand.

The object of this exercise is twofold. Firstly, it opens up the gaps behind the stone as much as possible, achieving a maximum bond with the pinner. Secondly, it will make certain that more of the surface area is sitting on the stone below.

applying downward pressure

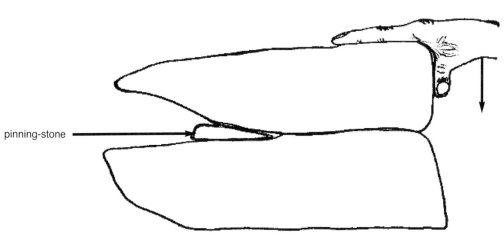

pinning-stone

Securing the face-stone to the wall.

It is important during this phase of construction to ensure that the wall is as level as possible to enable the course above to be laid securely. Due to the nature of random walling this cannot always be achieved by placing just one stone. On many occasions a few of the stones on the lower level will be varied in height. The only way to get around this problem, if a suitable sized stone cannot be found, is to build up the level with smaller face-stones.

Even if the top of a stone appears rounded, try to lay it with its widest and flattest side touching the course below.

This will ensure that it will fit on the wall with the minimum amount of movement. Any imperfections on the top can easily be overcome by building up the sides with smaller stone.

The properties of random stone dictate that sometime during the walling procedure awkward, concave joins will need to be bridged. Rather than just lay stones across the gaps, which will leave unsightly triangular crevices on the face of the wall, search for suitable candidates to match the shape required to bond the course. These stones can be thinner than the ones already in place, but have to be

To help create an even course, build up the sides of taller face-stones with smaller material. On the next course, the join will have to be bridged.

Building the course level.

long enough to penetrate towards the centre of the wall. Some limestone walls are built with the majority of stones locked together using angular joins.

Laying one skin of a course is relatively straightforward because the face-stone penetrates the wall's centre without too much trouble. The opposite side can prove trickier, often requiring specific sized materials due to the length of the stone protruding into the wall on the skin already built. The situation is exacerbated on the top courses where room becomes a premium because of the batter. The problem, however, is not just limited to the higher parts of the wall but can occur lower down, specifically when finishing a course near a wall-end if the

available stone is too wide to slot in the gap.

To overcome this problem the face-stone is trimmed to size with the chisel end of the walling hammer. It is quite a simple task that does not require exact accuracy. Simply judge the size needed to fit in the gap either by placing the face-stone on the wall and estimating how much will need to come off, or mark it out with a tape measure. Score a line with the chisel end of the walling hammer to highlight the amount to be cut off. Lift the stone off the wall and place it on level ground before cutting. Avoid working the front of the stone because it could create an uneven face.

Most stone will trim to size without too

Fitting an angular stone into an angular join.

Judging amount to be trimmed by placing stone on the wall.

Trimming the stone with a walling hammer.

Placing trimmed stone onto the wall.

much difficulty, but cutting weathered limestone and slate can prove to be a hit and miss affair due to the brittle nature of the rock. Instead of breaking where expected, they will often split down their fissures or bedding planes. This is highly frustrating, so every precaution should be taken to make sure the face-stone is sitting on a level surface, free of small stones and other foreign bodies, before it is hit with the hammer.

When the two skins of a course are complete, fill the centre with hearting. The hearting should not be thrown or poured into the wall, but inserted carefully by hand to protect the pinners under the face-stones. Now is the time to stand back and survey the work. Look down each course by standing at a wall-end and check the alignment of the face-stones in relation to the string-line and adjust any that are not parallel. Undertake this job after each course is completed.

The Through-Band

By the time the wall reaches the halfway mark, when all the lower courses are laid, at least half a ton of material per metre will be bearing down towards the foundation stones. At this stage the two skins of the wall can support themselves without too much trouble. When the wall reaches its full height the weight burden will have doubled, resulting in greater, uneven pressure on both sides of the wall. This imbalance could cause the wall to settle unevenly or, worst still, shift the lower face-stones so the wall begins to lean.

The idea behind the through-band is to bind the two skins on the lower courses together before extra weight is applied to the wall. The weight produced by the higher face-stones, once it is absorbed by the through-band, will distribute itself on a more even keel, transferring the load to all of the stones below.

Before laying the through-band, bring the existing course of face-stones as level as possible and then raise the string-lines out of the way to enable clear access to the wall. Most through-stones are heavy and may require two people to handle them in order to avoid the risk of serious injury when they are lifted. These stones are not usually stored immediately adjacent to the work site. Carrying a heavy through-stone some distance to the wall could place considerable strain on the arms resulting in the stone being dropped

The through-band is a single course of wall, running horizontally through the centre, where through-stones are placed every 3–4ft (90–120cm) along the wall.

through-stones

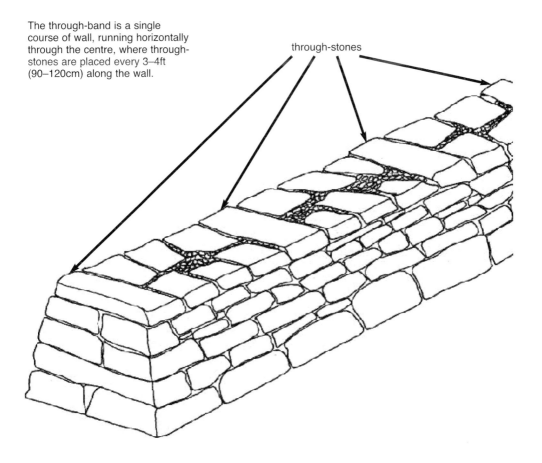

The through-band.

onto and damaging the course below.

Lay the through-stones every 3–4ft (90–120cm) along the course with their flattest and widest sides resting on the stones below. Pinning-stones will not be required, but fill any gaps underneath with hearting. If the stone is longer than the width of the course, move it so that the point of balance is resting on the centre, even if it means that both ends protrude out of the wall. It has long been recognized by the dry stone walling community that these stones are difficult to cut, especially if the material is brittle. It is far better to break the aesthetics of a smooth face than to break an important through-stone down the wrong fissure. The same can be said for the end-stones once the wall's batter becomes narrow.

Building the Upper Courses

If the string-lines have been moved to accommodate the through-band, reset them to just above the highest stones on the course. Concentrate on building the gaps between each through-stone, bringing the wall as level as possible. To enhance the effect of this section lay face-stones that will be able to penetrate the centre and rest on the hearting. Try to achieve this on both sides, but if the supply of adequate, sized stone is limited, place them at equal intervals along the course then fill the centre with hearting.

Constructing the top half of the wall follows the exact same principles as the lower section, with a couple of exceptions.

Levelling the wall ready for the through-band.

The through-band.

The top courses on the majority of walls are made up
of small face-stones.

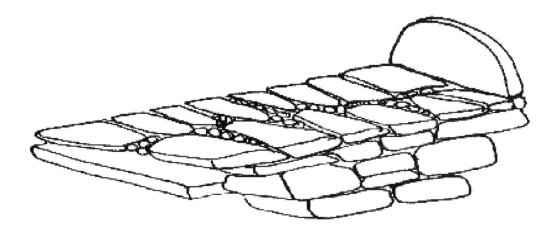

The cover-band helps to tie the two skins at the top
of the wall together. In most cases ideal stone is not
available. If this is the case, use the method shown
above.

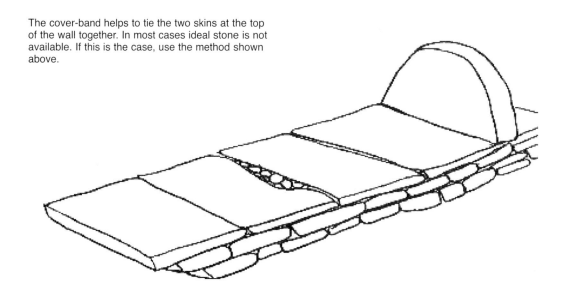

The last course of face-stones.

Firstly, there is a fundamental contrast of convenient surface area to build on, which could result in more hammer work on the stones. Secondly, as the wall begins to reach full height the quantity of walling material decreases. The latter may end in frustration when searching for an ideal face-stone and an uncertainty of the amount of material left to finish the job may creep in also. If the quantities of random walling have been worked out properly before the start of the job, 1 ton per metre of a wall built to the height of 4ft 6in (1.4m), there should be no problem.

Start building on the through-band after raising the string-lines no more than 5in (12cm) above the course. Lay the end-stones first then effect a level course by laying the face-stones in between, utilizing the same method as already detailed for the lower half of the wall. A further through-band can be laid halfway between the first band and the estimated finished level. In truth, this is an unrealistic option because in most cases ideal through-stones are fairly scarce. Do not worry about the second through-band if the stones are not available.

The last few courses of face-stone should consist of smaller material. If there is any large material left over at this stage, it can be broken up with a sledge hammer in order to produce the ideal size of stone needed. The concluding course is the most critical because it could contain very small stone that will have to sustain the initial weight of the coping-stones. All of the face-stones, without exception, must be laid with their lengths protruding into the centre, with each one tightly abutted against its neighbour. Stone that is placed with its longest face to the front will pivot out when the wall

settles. This will disturb the coping and result in the premature decay of the courses.

The Coping-Stones

The layer of coping-stones acts as the wall's first shield of defence against the ravages of nature and damage by livestock and human beings. The course of coping seals the top of the wall by spanning the two skins and binding them together. A wall that lacks coping will deteriorate course by course, section by section, undoing the hard work it has taken to build it. No dry stone structure should be left unprotected without these stones on the top. In relation to the remainder of the wall these stones are more exposed and as a result they tend to weather rapidly. If coping is dislodged it forms a gap that will gradually increase in size until repair work is required.

Types of coping can vary and are not governed by regional styles. It is good practice, however, to copy the characteristics of the walls in the immediate locality of any given work site. Upright stones, locked tightly together to form continuous, unbroken lines are the most common forms. These are usually found on field boundary walls.

Start the coping by laying the end-stones first. Preferably these should be similar in height and entirely self-supporting, so they can rest on the wall without having to be pinned. Two, strong coping-stones, at either end of the course, will act like bookends for the ones in-between.

Once the two end-stones are on, a string-line can be used as a guide for the height of the finished course. Tie the line

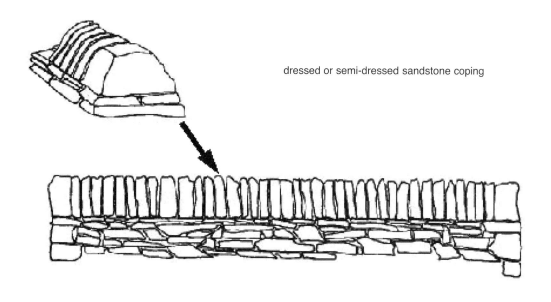

dressed or semi-dressed sandstone coping

typical, uneven limestone coping

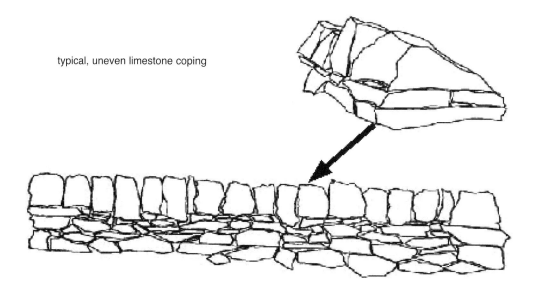

Popular styles of coping-stone in Britain (1).

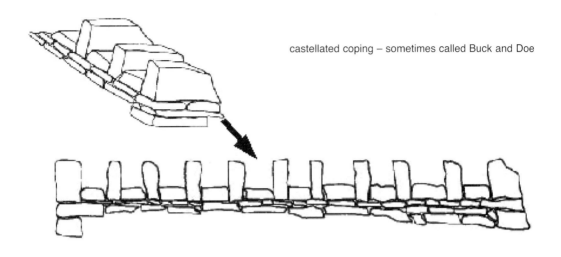

castellated coping – sometimes called Buck and Doe

coping-stone on a retaining wall

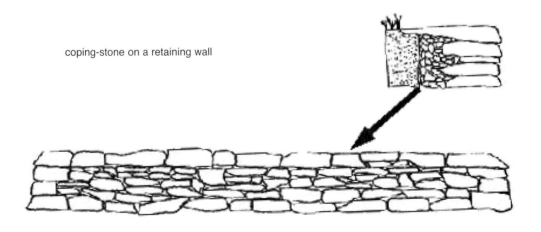

Popular styles of coping-stone in Britain (2).

to a pin and insert it into a crevice in one of the wall-ends. Stretch the string over the top of the coping-stone and pull it tightly over the top of the other one. Again, anchor the line in the wall-end. On longer stretches of wall, a third coping-stone can be placed halfway down the course to prevent the string-line from sagging.

Work from one end and place each coping-stone firmly against its neighbour, making sure that the fit is as tight as possible. Above all, its full weight will need to rest on the face-stones on each side of the course. If the coping-stone requires pinning, it should be inserted from the side facing down the course and pushed completely underneath to ensure the next stone laid up against it will sit securely on the wall.

If an aesthetic look is required, work to the height of the top string-line. Parts of the top course can be raised with extra face-stones, pinned and filled with hearting, to bed-in smaller coping-stones. If the coping has not become brittle due to the effects of weathering, trim any stone that overhangs the face, flush with the wall. If, however, the priority is stock proofing, uneven coping will help to deter sheep from climbing or jumping the wall.

The string-line attached ready for the coping-stones.

Inserting a pinner under a coping-stone, ensuring that it is pushed firmly underneath.

The completed wall; note the uneven coping to discourage livestock.

CHAPTER 5

BUILDING OR REPAIRING
A CURVED WALL

Curves are useful as an aesthetic feature or when there is a need to direct a wall past an obstacle such as a mature tree.

Building a curve can seem daunting to the uninitiated. Although the construction technique is exactly the same as one would use for a straight length of wall, it is virtually impossible to build it using permanent batter-frames and string-lines as guides. Instead, a customized frame can be used at certain points during the construction phases. The fact that these guides are unavailable will mean that the foundation trench and the courses below are the only point of reference to aid the walls' batter and shape. This requires the waller to keep a constant check on the line using his or her eyesight.

The last feature a craftsman will want to build is an uneven, bulging wall. Therefore to achieve a good result it pays to be diligent, constantly checking the position of each stone in relation to the rest of the wall and adjusting for the curve and batter where necessary. The technique is not as difficult as it sounds. All the waller has to do is lay the face-stone a few millimetres further into the centre of the wall than the one placed on the bottom. Once one has achieved a few

courses using this method, confidence to carry on will come quickly.

The project for this section involves the reconstruction of a damaged wall that pre-dates the Enclosures Act. The wall has collapsed due to a collision with a lorry, which obliterated a wall-end and displaced a large number of face-stones. Not only will the damaged section need to be reconstructed to form a curve, the new part of the wall will have to resemble the style of the surrounding area.

Extra Tool Requirements

• A customized batter-frame: this is a frame consisting of two batter sides and one top baton. The top baton should equate to the width of the wall at coping-stone height.

Preparation Work

On projects like this the first important job is to assess the amount of walling stone available and place it in piles or graded rows near to the walling site. To help create a safe working area, concentrate on the stone already scattered on

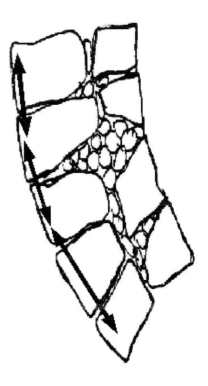

Lay the stones for the curve by using the course below as a template. (The arrows represent the next course of face-stones to be placed on top.)

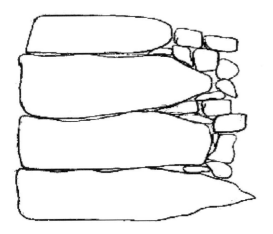

When building without the aid of a string-line, set the face-stone 1in (2cm) in from the one on the lower course. After the course is finished, check the alignment by eye and adjust if needed. Check any suspect areas with the customized batter-frame.

Laying the face-stone for the curve.

the ground. Look initially for suitable stones for the wall-ends and the through-band. Place them to one side for later use. Next, concentrate on the coping-stones. Use the existing walls in the area as a guide for the style required and place suitable candidates on one side also. Now, carefully remove obviously loose stones from the top of the wall that could be of hazard to the waller or the general public and place them on the relevant pile or row.

As soon as it is safe to proceed further, the task of assessing the damage to the collapsed area can be undertaken. First, check the state of the face-stones on the remaining courses of wall. Due to the type of impact on the project wall, it must be assumed that the lorry has caused a vast amount of unseen damage. As a precaution, each remaining course within this area will have to be dismantled down to the foundations.

Start removing the courses by lifting the stones slowly and vertically off the wall, one at a time. Take down each individual course in turn, placing the face-stones on their relevant piles or rows.

As each course is dismantled the intact part of the wall will need to be stepped, in order for the new section to tie in effectively. This will mean having to remove a

Badly damaged wall showing the dangerous loose stones.

Grading the stone in ordered rows.

Lifting stone off the wall vertically. Dragging stone could cause the structure to collapse.

substantial amount of face-stone from the good wall. The procedure can be dangerous in older features that contain small material. Injuries due to collapses of otherwise strong sections of wall are common if the correct methods are not followed. Each stepped section must be created with the utmost care and attention, for they will need to be secured, ready to safely accept the new wall. This is highlighted by the fact that this part of the wall will be exposed for a considerable amount of time – sometimes days. Therefore it is imperative the exposed courses remain sturdy through the duration of the job.

The main danger arises when part of the face-stone to be removed is tied under a section of wall that is staying in place. Before the stone can be safely handled, the one sitting on top will need to be propped with temporary wedges, jammed into the centre of the wall. Once these wedges are able to take the weight, the stone can be slowly moved out of position.

Laying the Foundation

Use the base of the existing wall as a guide for the width of the foundation trench and transfer this measurement to where the new wall-end is to be built. Mark the area with two stones, or two

If this stone were removed at this point the wall could collapse.

Ramming temporary wedges into the wall to prop up existing courses.

The stone can now be removed safely.

Digging foundations to required depth; note how the existing wall is stepped ready for the repaired section to be tied in.

small pins or stakes. To create the template for the curve, use two lengths of rope and run them out on the ground on both sides of the existing wall, up to the markers for the new wall-end. Move the ropes until they represent a smooth, sweeping curve. The width between the two ropes will need to be the same width as the base of the wall. This can be adjusted using the tape measure.

Using the ropes as a guide, mark out the shape of the trench, on both sides, with a spade. Depending on the depth of topsoil, excavate the trench to the required depth. This could be anything between 6in (15cm) to 12in (30cm) deep. Try to keep the edges vertical. When complete, level the trench by walking up and down it several times. Firm up any soft areas by ramming in small stones with a sledge hammer or tamper.

Start the foundation course by setting in the stones for the new wall-end. These can either be a through or two runners. Lay the rest of the foundation stones using the curved trench as the template. The best results will be achieved if the stones are placed tightly against the sides of the trench, utilizing it as a template. Finish the course by filling with hearting.

Moving the foundation stones into the trench.

The completed foundations.

Building the Lower Courses

Commence the first course of face-stones by tying it into the existing wall on both sides. Depending on the type of stone used for the foundation, lay a through or runners on the wall-end. Employing the foundation course as a guide for the curve, build up the face-stone between the wall-end and existing wall, pinning each stone as it is used. Once a course is tied into the existing wall, any temporary wedges can be removed. Finish the course by filling the centre with hearting.

Stop the walling process and take time out to look down the line of the wall. Check the curvature on both sides of the wall and from both ends. Scrutinize each face-stone and adjust any that are out of alignment. There is no need to check the batter at this stage.

Build up the next course the same as the one below by tying into the existing wall, placing the end-stones and laying the face-stones in-between, using the course below as the template for the curve. Check the alignment of face-stones in relation to the curve and adjust as necessary.

Tying the new wall into the existing structure.

Adjusting the stones to follow the curve. Note how all the face-stones are laid with their length into the wall.

From this point onwards the batter has to be checked. Slot the customized batter-frame over the wall at intervals along the courses. To achieve a near accurate batter the frame should touch the bottom of the wall on both sides. It must be noted that this method is not totally accurate and it is really up to the wallers' skilful eye to obtain the best results. The frame will have to be removed before initiating the next course of wall.

Build subsequent courses exactly the same as the lower ones. Lay a through-band halfway up the wall, making sure that the through-stones tie the two skins together. Bring the rest of the course level with the through-band, remembering to tie in the new wall with the existing one.

Construct a further two or three courses working with the same method as described in the previous chapter, stopping one course below the coping-stones. The next course of face-stones will be the base for the coping. Since it has not been possible to use string-lines as a guide to level the wall earlier in the project, it is essential to ensure that the course of coping-stones are correctly levelled. In order to do this properly it is advisable to set up a string-line.

A customized batter-frame can be used to check the batter of the wall, but it will have to be removed before laying further face-stones.

The bottom baton is removed so it can be placed over the wall.

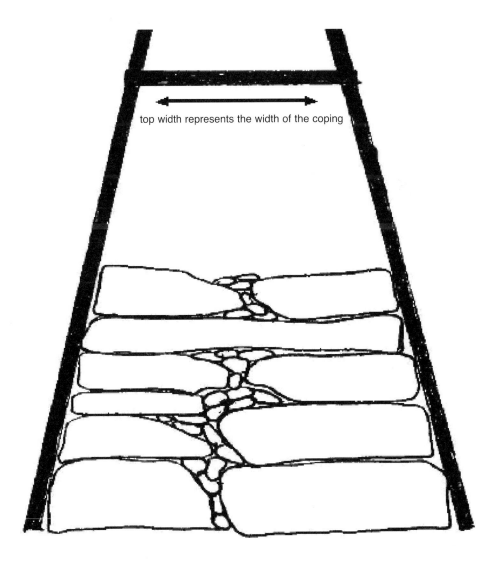

top width represents the width of the coping

When checking the batter the frame should be touching the faces of the wall.

Using a customized batter-frame for the curve.

Levelling the wall ready for the through-band.

The through-band showing the through-stones bridging both skins of the wall.

String-line set up to ensure that the coping is level.

It is impossible for the line to follow the exact curve of the wall; the nearest solution is to set up the string at an obtuse angle. Attach the string by wrapping it two or three times around the first coping-stone on the existing wall. Before running the line out to the arc of the curve, make sure the string is jammed between the wall and the base of the coping. Next, tie the string-line around a normal face-stone and place the stone on the wall, at the arc of the curve. Now pull the string toward the wall-end. To secure the line the batter-frame can be set up beyond the wall-end and the line can be tied to the frame's baton.

The Coping-Stones

The coping-stone on the wall-end should be a large free-standing stone. Lay the rest of the coping in keeping with the existing wall, making sure that each one is tightly locked to the other (*see* Chapter 4 for the method of laying coping-stone). Work until the new section has been successfully tied to the rest of the wall.

The completed curved wall, blended in with the surroundings.

Viewing the completed structure from a different angle, showing the wall-end.

Carrying out Repairs on a Straight Wall which includes a Wall-End

It is easier to repair a straight wall than a curved one, in that it is possible to use string-lines and a batter-frame. Follow the instructions detailed earlier in this chapter for dismantling the damaged courses and ensure that there are a series of steps created ready to accept the new face-stones. Prepare the foundations as described in Chapter 4. The batter-frame can be set up at the wall-end with the string-lines secured by pins inserted into the undamaged courses of the wall under repair. The techniques used to reconstruct the section are the same basic techniques outlined in Chapter 4.

Building a Corner

Where a wall reaches a ninety-degree intersection, as on a square enclosure, the corners will have to be secured. Rather than build an excessive amount of wall-ends, or use up too much stone by adding curves, large stones can be laid in such a manner that they tie the two, meeting walls together.

The weakest part of the structure is

the outside skin, due to the fact that the stone is exposed on two faces. Strong runners, bridging every join without exception, should be used to build up the entire section. The inside face is slightly stronger because at least half of the stone is inserted inside both walls; therefore the chances of them pivoting out are very slim. The last diagram in this chapter describes this method in greater detail.

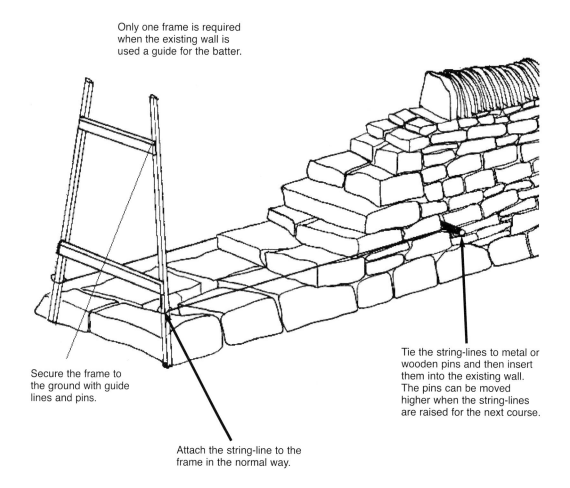

Only one frame is required when the existing wall is used a guide for the batter.

Secure the frame to the ground with guide lines and pins.

Attach the string-line to the frame in the normal way.

Tie the string-lines to metal or wooden pins and then insert them into the existing wall. The pins can be moved higher when the string-lines are raised for the next course.

Using a batter-frame for repairing an existing wall.

a heavy, free-standing coping-stone placed on the corner

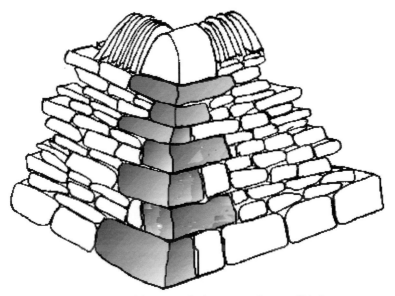

The outside face of the corner is the one most susceptible to damage. Runners, depicted by the shaded stone, will form a strong buttress.

Secure these stones by bridging this join.

Bridge this join.

inside face

These two stones will be bridged on the next course.

outside face

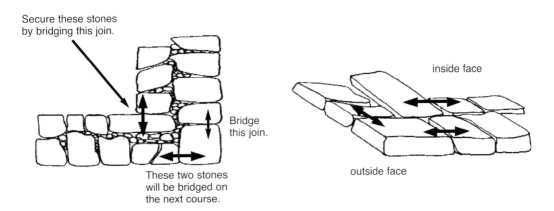

Corner section.

CHAPTER 6

WALLING ON SLOPES

It takes far less energy to roll a rock down hill than to roll it up. It is for this reason that gravity plays a major role when building walls on slopes. A dry stone wall built on level ground could last for hundreds of years – even one containing mistakes. On hillsides, these mistakes can produce devastating effects, resulting in a constant, expensive, gapping regime. This is not due to the difficulties of building walls against the direction of gravity; it is purely down to bad walling technique. With some common-sense changes in the basic walling method these problems can be easily overcome.

A popular error is to lay the face-stones leaning up the slope. Surprisingly, this is quite common on older walls. It is obvious that if the wall is built in this way the stones will eventually slide downhill, as they often do. One has to bear in mind that a twenty-metre long wall could contain at least twenty tons of material. This is a vast amount of weight when perched on the side of a mountain with the laws of physics dictating that the natural path of this mass is downward.

The damaging effect of gravity can be greatly reduced by laying the wall's courses as level as possible. This way some of the energy is transferred vertically through the wall, enabling each face-stone to absorb the weight, greatly reducing the pressure at the bottom of the slope. A correctly built, vertical wall-end will enhance the strength of the wall by forming a solid buttress that is able to absorb and dissipate the remaining energy safely. In fact, the ideal way to build on a slope is to construct small sections at a time, each containing their own wall-ends.

Extra tool requirements

- 4 metal rods for use as batter-frames.
- 1 customized batter-frame, the same as the one used in Chapter 5.

Working Out the Levels and Setting Up the Batter

Always start the wall at the foot of a slope, on level ground if possible. The first job is to measure the width of the foundation trench (*see* Chapter 4). Take two of the metal rods and insert them at each of the two points, making sure that they are set up with the correct batter for the wall. The customized batter-frame can be used as a template when knocking the rods into the ground. With the rods firmly in place, tie on a string-line at coping-stone height. If there are no other walls in the area to take this measurement from, work to the standard height of 4ft 6in (1.4m).

Take the other end of the line and walk it up the slope to a point where it meets the ground and the string appears level to the eye. At this point, pull the line taut. The line level can now be attached to the string, somewhere near the centre. Adjust the string by moving it up or down the slope until the line level's bubble settles between its two marks. Insert the next two rods here, making sure they are the same width apart as the ones below. Use the wooden frame again to adjust the rods to the correct batter. The string now represents the top of the wall-end at the bottom of the slope, and shows us where the foundation stone for the next wall-end

should be placed. For the time being do not secure it to any of the rods.

This part of the exercise has ensured that a strong, level wall can now be erected between the two sets of rods. The actual length of the proposed wall section will be governed by the angle of the slope. The steeper the hill, the shorter each section of wall will be.

Using the same string-line, tie it 4ft 6in (1.4m) from ground level, on to one of the rods on the slope. The line is now an accurate guide for the top of the wall and should remain in place throughout the construction phase.

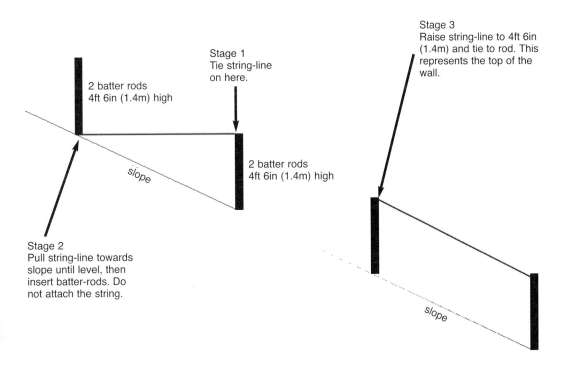

Securing the string-line.

Laying the Foundations

The foundations for this type of wall are laid in a sequence of steps, with the higher stones always bridging the ones below. It is important, however, to make sure that each foundation stone is below ground level, so a normal excavation of the whole trench, following the angle of the hill, should be implemented first (*see* Chapter 4). When the trench is finished, level shelves can then be cut for each individual part of the foundation.

Working from the bottom of the hill, excavate a level shelf for the first foundation stones. A spirit level can be used to determine an even platform. If the stone is going to be a through, make sure it is large and heavy. If they are to be runners, choose the longest, thickest ones. As a precaution, check these with the spirit level when they are in place and adjust the ground underneath if necessary. Do not insert pinners to level the stones. Next, cut out a second, level shelf directly above the first stones then manoeuvre two more foundations into place. Make sure they are level and they bridge the stones below by at least 5in (12cm). Continue building the foundations in same manner up to the second set of rods. At this point, lay throughs or runners for the next wall-end. Once all the foundation stones are firm, fill the centre of the wall with large hearting.

Building the Lower Courses

The wall is now ready for the first courses of level face-stones. To help achieve this, the customized batter-frame can be slotted over the wall and moved up the slope as and when required. Do not worry if the top string-line seems to get in the way, just place the frame over the top. The string's elasticity will help it to bend with the weight. To prevent the frame from moving it can be secured at the base with large stones used as props against its batter-rails and tied with an easy release knot to the top string-line.

Place the frame either side of the wall, at a point near to where the third set of foundation stones bridges the ones below. Next, tie the string-lines at ground level to both sides of the frame then attach them to the rods at the bottom wall-end. Make sure that the strings are level. The area running between the strings now represents the first course of wall to be built.

No matter how small this area appears, do not be tempted to build higher than the string-lines. It is vital, for the strength of the wall, that each stone is level, using these lines as an accurate template.

To lay the next course, remove the batter-frame and secure it at the next join of the foundation stones. Tie the strings at ground level and then adjust them on the bottom rods with the aid of the line level. Build this course using the same method as described for the first. The only factor that will change is the length of each course as the wall is built higher. Continue erecting the wall in this way until the bottom wall-end is complete.

Building the Upper Courses

As the next courses of wall are laid into place they will include the stones for the second wall-end. At this stage, the bottom

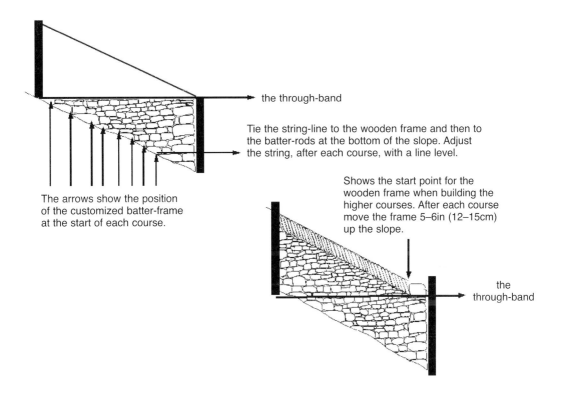

the through-band

Tie the string-line to the wooden frame and then to the batter-rods at the bottom of the slope. Adjust the string, after each course, with a line level.

The arrows show the position of the customized batter-frame at the start of each course.

Shows the start point for the wooden frame when building the higher courses. After each course move the frame 5–6in (12–15cm) up the slope.

the through-band

Building the different stages of wall.

batter-rods will become redundant, but will still have to remain in position to keep the top string-line secure. Attention is now turned toward the second set of rods already in position further up the slope. These will be used in conjunction with the wooden frame and string-lines to help create level courses of face-stone for the next phase of the job.

Working from the bottom of the slope, slot the frame over both sides of the wall. Secure it 5in (12cm) in from the wall-end. Tie the strings to the frame, 5in above the last course of face-stone, and then attach them to the second set of batter-rods, making sure the string is taut and level.

Build this next course of wall as the through-band (*see* Chapter 4).

After the through-band has been placed, move the wooden frame a further 5–6in (12–15cm) up the slope and immobilize it with large stones propped up against the batter-rails, making sure both rails are touching the two skins of wall. Just moving the frame this short distance will make sure that the string-lines can be raised above the wall, allowing for accurate placing of face-stones. Again, use the line level when adjusting the string-lines on the batter-rods and then lay the next course. Repeat this procedure for all the subsequent courses until the second wall-end is constructed. By this time the top should resemble a flight of level of steps. These steps will be of great use when the coping is placed on the wall.

The Coping-Stones

The coping-stones on this type of wall are laid differently to those built on level ground. The stones are placed so that they lean up the slope. This changes their centre of gravity to ensure that they won't topple down the hill, but are still an effective bond for the top of the wall. The only stones that need to be vertical are the large freestanding ones at the start and end of the feature.

Apart from these differences, the coping is secured to the wall in the same way as any other – tightly locked together and bridging the two skins of wall (*see* Chapter 4). The string-line that represents the top of the wall can now be used as a guide for the height of the coping.

Continuing Up the Slope

Build another complete wall by simply repeating all of the steps described in this chapter, making sure that where the wall-ends meet they are tightly butted together, and the join running from top to bottom is bridged with a large coping stone.

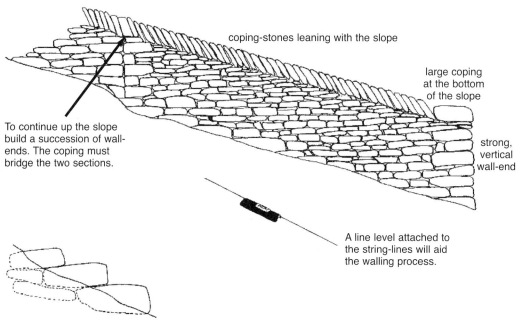

coping-stones leaning with the slope

large coping
at the bottom
of the slope

To continue up the slope build a succession of wall-ends. The coping must bridge the two sections.

strong,
vertical
wall-end

A line level attached to the string-lines will aid the walling process.

The foundations are laid in steps.

Walling up the slope.

CHAPTER 7

GAPPING

To *gap* a wall or the process of *gapping* defines the task of repairing a decayed or decaying part of a dry stone wall. The initial stage of this job could turn out to be fairly hazardous as it involves the handling of insecure stone that, at any moment, could collapse around your feet. A decayed wall will require an inspection to determine the extent of damage and, most importantly, the possible hazard to the waller whose job it is to repair it.

Treat the wall like a house of cards and work out how each stone can be safely removed without causing a major collapse. Inspect the joins and the way that the face-stones bridge them, with the purpose of establishing how the remaining wall can be dismantled from top to bottom and course by course.

Try to establish what factors caused the wall to be damaged in the first place. It is no good rebuilding the gap if the source of the problem is not eliminated. Look for the obvious signs. A bulging wall could be the result of face-stones that have collapsed in the centre because of eroded hearting. Flooding or a stream could have caused this erosion. If there are mature trees in the vicinity, their root systems may be impacting the foundations (*see* Chapter 9 for a technique that could resolve the predicament of tree roots or running water).

Almost all damage will result in the movement of a significant quantity of pinning and hearting resulting in the main stones on the wall being tenuously connected to the main structure. It is expected that walls in this state would have tumbled down already, but always treat a damaged wall with the utmost respect. The motto here is to expect the unexpected. The obvious way of gaining information about reasons for the wall's demise is to speak to the landowner.

Types of Damage

Vehicle collision is common, but the damage is usually restricted to the impact area due to the flexibility of the courses on dry stone wall. In many scenarios it is the car or van that has sustained the greater damage. It has been known for a wall to basically stay in one piece whilst the front end of the motor vehicle has become a crumpled wreck. This isn't to say that it will not need repairing, for an impact such as this will dislodge face-stones and their important pinning-stones.

Livestock can also start the decay process, with sheep trying to climb the top or cattle rubbing against the faces. Walkers taking short cuts across fields

Wall damaged by tree growth.

Gap caused by theft of stones.

are the cause of a substantial amount of damage. Quite often, when a wall is scaled, the coping will move or be pushed off. This leaves the important top section open to rain and frosts.

The one form of damage that saddens any dry stone waller is theft. Thieves play a major role in stealing valuable stone and where the countryside borders urban districts this continues to be a very serious problem.

Assessing the Damaged Wall

The project wall for this chapter forms part of a sandstone field boundary where a quantity of stone has been stolen. Looking at the way the gap has been dismantled it would appear that the thieves knew exactly where and how to take the stones, because it has been left stepped. This does not mean that they thought they would do the landowner a favour and leave it in such a state that rebuilding would be made easier. On the contrary, these were professional thieves and they knew how to take the stone off the wall without causing a major collapse. Although they have made the job of reconstruction easier it does not change the fact that these people broke the law and if caught they could face prosecution.

The assumption to be made, as with any damage associated with theft of dry stone walling material, is that there will be serious lack of stone on site. The first job is to look around the immediate work area for any original stone that can be salvaged. It is not a good idea to take the stone from other parts of the wall as this only leads to obvious rebuilding problems in the future. Luckily, in this case, the coping-stone was taken off the wall and left in the field, evidently too heavy for the thieves to handle in any quantity.

Having determined the amount of

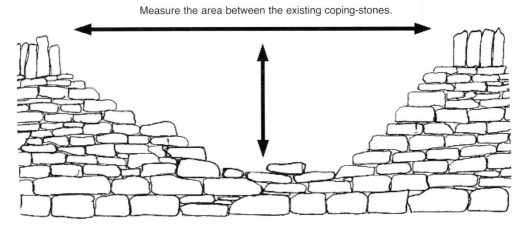

Measure the area between the existing coping-stones.

Measure the area from the bottom of the wall
up to the height of the coping-stones.

Measuring the gap for the stone.

stone available for rebuilding, the next job is to measure the gap. With a tape measure, work out the length of the missing section between the existing coping-stones then measure from ground level to the height of where the coping should be. Work on the equation that a wall requires one ton of stone for every metre length built to 4ft 6in (1.4m) high and transpose this equation to suit the size of the gap.

Preparing the Wall

The initial job to carry out, before laying the stone, is to clear away loose hearting and debris from the wall and store them to one side for later use. Next, check the stability of the existing wall on both sides of the gap. Any slight movement can be dealt with by inserting pinners behind the stone, but if excess movement is detected the stone will have to be removed and the area underneath it cleared of debris. If the sides of the gap are vertical, they will need to be stepped to tie in the new stone (*see* Chapter 5 for the procedure for creating safe steps).

The important stones are the ones at the bottom. This is where the gap will be built up from, so they will need to be secure. Remove these stones and clear away any debris from the face-stones they were sitting on. Continue removing courses until a solid, tight bed is reached, even if it means replacing the foundation stones.

Clearing loose debris from the wall.

Rebuilding the Gap

The same, basic walling technique applies to this phase as described throughout Chapter 4, except that batter-frames will not be required. Instead of templates set up at both ends, two string-lines are inserted into the faces of the existing wall each side of the gap and raised after each course is complete. It is worth a mention, however, that experienced craftsmen usually dispense with guiding lines if the gap is very small and rely on their skilful eye to align the courses.

To guarantee a long-lasting bond, each course of the gap will have to be tied to both sides of the old wall. This action is essential if the new face-stones are going to last the life of the wall.

If access to the other side of the wall is difficult, resulting in it being necessary to build both skins of the wall from the same side, begin by laying the opposite face. By doing this first the face-stones can be manoeuvred and pinned without disturbing the row of stones directly in front of the waller. An experienced waller is able to judge the alignment of the face-stones on the opposite side, by looking at the alignment of the stone and feeling the face with a hand and adjusting it in relation to the lower course.

Working to the basic procedures described in Chapter 4, build the gap to the last course, remembering to tie it into the old wall and making sure that each face-stone is pinned where needed and the centres are filled with hearting. To achieve a level finish with the coping, attach a string-line to the coping-stones either side of the gap exactly as described in Chapter 4.

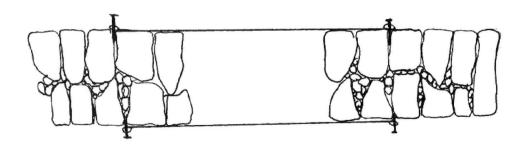

String-lines are attached to pins then inserted into the crevices of the wall. Make sure the strings are touching the fronts of the existing face-stones. This will help to achieve the correct batter. Raise the strings when each course is completed.

Using string-lines as a guide for the batter.

Laying opposite face-stones first when walling from one side.

Laying near side face-stones once the opposite face-stones are in place.

Laying a face-stone, ensuring the joins are bridged.

After each course fill the centre with hearting.

Two large through-stones forming the through-band.

Levelling the wall ready for the coping-stones.

Placing the coping-stone, ensuring that the stone bridges the two gaps before securing in place with pinning-stone.

CHAPTER 8

RETAINING WALLS

Retaining walls are used primarily for supporting unstable soil banks, which otherwise may subside due the effect of erosion. The height of this style of wall is governed by the size of soil bank behind and could range from as little as 1ft (30cm) to as much as 10ft (3m) and higher. Out of all the walling styles this is probably the most popular, especially with the enthusiastic gardener, as it can be used to create ornamental garden features. On average, there are more retaining dry stone walls built than any other style.

The construction principles remain the same for this wall as for a double-skinned wall: laying large stone at the base, building even courses of pinned face-stone, erecting strong wall-ends and finishing with a row of coping. All retaining walls, without exception, have to be built with a batter. Without this, any movement of the soil structure behind could push the wall over. The major role of the batter is to help counter the force of the soil bank on the wall by spreading this energy through each face-stone before it is released at the foundation course.

There is one fundamental difference that sets this type of wall apart from any other; it only requires one skin of face-stones and thus the importance of the batter cannot be emphasized enough.

The project wall for this chapter was especially chosen to demonstrate a number of significant points. Firstly, it will show how not to build a wall, as the original wall was poorly constructed. Secondly, it is an example of what happens when the face-stones are laid without prior thought to the substantial weight of soil pushing from behind. Lastly, by laying the exact same stone in the correct way, it will serve as an example to show how random stone can be applied to form an attractive long-lasting feature.

By careful scrutiny of the original wall, we can determine the reason for this features' unkempt appearance. The first faults that are prominent are the lack of coping-stones, the unevenness of the entire structure and the rough-looking fronts of the face-stones. A subsequent study of the wall will reveal that many of the face-stones do not project toward the soil bank and the wall has a vertical face. Further investigations expose the fact that only a minority of face-stone was pinned, there was a distinct lack of hearting and the through-band was nowhere to be seen. All of this, coupled with the weight of the bank it was meant to support, has resulted in the wall becoming structurally dangerous to the point of collapse.

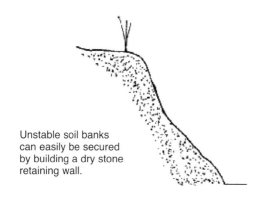

Unstable soil banks can easily be secured by building a dry stone retaining wall.

Create an even slope by digging away excess soil and rubble. Next, excavate a foundation trench along the entire length of the proposed wall.

A retaining wall is similar to any other dry stone wall, except it only requires one side of walling stone. Note also how it leans into the bank so that its weight is forced toward the area that needs to be retained. The wall could only fall backwards.

The coping should bridge the entire area of wall with the back of the stones resting on the bank.

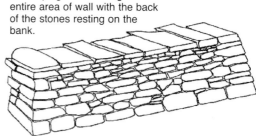

Like a double-sided dry stone wall, a retaining wall needs to be sealed by wall-ends. Secure each stone in the normal way by pinners. Fill the space between the bank and the back of the stones with hearting. Note how the length of the stones is projecting into the wall.

The finished wall. Note how the coping-stone is placed with the greater surface area on the wall.

Dry stone retaining wall.

The project before commencement of repairs.

Extra Tool Requirements

• 2 or 3 batter-rods instead of wooden frames

Dismantling the Old Wall

Unsafe walls like this ought to be disassembled, one course at a time, storing the stone within easy reach of the work site. It is safe to assume with a bad wall that the foundations will be incapable of supporting the wall's weight, so they should be removed and the foundation trench re-excavated. In the case of the project wall, the hard surface of the steps it was built on formed an ideal foundation and no excavation work was needed.

After removing the stones, dig the bank away until the soil becomes firm. If the soil structure is too soft, the wall will collapse backwards.

Before reconstruction, it is necessary to insert the batter-rods at either end of the proposed wall. Usually, small lengths of retaining wall only require two, one at either end. Where a long section of wall is to be constructed a third rod can be inserted halfway between the two to stop the string-line from sagging. The project wall required three because of the change in height created by the steps.

Hammer the rods into the ground with a lump hammer, at the same time adjusting them for the batter. The angle can be anything from one-in-four to one-in-six. Tie an end of the string-line to one of

Preparing for the foundations, the batter-rods and string-line in place.

the rods, about 2in (5cm) off the ground, then tie the other end to the next rod, pulling it as tight as possible. Again, 2in (5cm) from ground level. The photograph depicts a second, higher string-line. This is the guide for the top of the wall. It is an optional feature at this stage, but serves as a useful tool to check the accuracy of the batter. To inspect the batter, stand behind one of the rods and look directly down the string-lines. If the two strings are travelling in different directions, one appearing to go left and the other to the right, the batter is wrong. Correct it by adjusting the angles of the rods until the strings run a parallel course.

Building the Wall

Lay the end-stones first. They must project into the bank, sealing the ends of the course. Align the front of the stone so it runs parallel and just touches the string. Try not to push the string-line out of alignment. Lay the remaining foundation stones in the trench with their lengths projecting toward the bank. Butt the sides of each stone together, minimizing the gaps between the joins. Finish the course by inserting hearting behind the stones.

Begin the next course by raising the string-line 3–4in (7–10cm) on the batter-

The through-stones; note how they are inserted into the bank.

rods, then lift the next end-stones on the wall. Wall-ends on a retaining wall are built in exactly the same way as on a double-skinned wall, using the same pattern of alternate throughs and runners. The only difference is that the runners at the back of the wall bridge over to the hearting as opposed to the second skin. Through-stones should be laid so the back is inserted into the bank or, at least, touching it.

Build the next course of face-stones, inserting pinners when needed and adjusting their fronts in accordance with the string-line. Backfill with hearting, taking care not to disturb the pinning-stone. Continue in the same fashion until half of the wall is constructed; this will be the height of the through-band.

The through-band on a retaining wall is designed to bind the lower half of wall to the soil bank. Through-stones are laid on the course then literally dug into the soil. The wall, in effect, then becomes part of the bank.

Once the through-band is secured the rest of the course can be brought level. On the project wall the course following the through-band raised it to the height of the step, which involved having to tie the foundation of this section to the courses already under construction. The two sections of wall had to be joined together to create one single feature and

Bridging the join between the lower part of the wall and the step.

Foundation stones laid on the step.

was easily achieved by simply laying the foundations over the step and onto the wall. Once the new foundations were in place, the rest of the walling procedure was identical to the previous courses.

The Coping-Stones

Before laying the coping a retaining wall should be built just below the level of the top bank – 1in (2.5cm) is sufficient. The reason for this is because the top of the soil bank will need to be dug away to produce a level area for the coping to sit on. This helps to minimize the possibility of future movement of the coping-stones.

Although there are some styles of retaining wall which host a vertical coping, on walls that may be subjected to climbing or seating activities, the coping is best laid with its greater surface area to the wall. A flat stone will even out any weight that could be applied if the wall is walked on, consequently protecting the courses below.

Before laying the coping, check the level of the top string-line with a line level or, if one is confident, by eye. Using this string-line as a guide lay the coping-stones so their tops just brush the string. Adjust the stones until their fronts are parallel with the rest of the wall. Raise the height of any coping-stone that appears angled along the front face, by

The coping-stones are laid horizontally to tie the wall into the bank.

The completed retaining wall.

inserting a thin face-stone underneath to bring it level. The small stone will, of course, need pinning and the gaps created underneath the coping should be filled with small hearting.

Finally, finish the wall by ramming in soil or turf between the gaps of the coping on the soil bank. Refrain from doing this on the wall as it may unsettle the stones below. Eventually, when the vegetation grows back, it will help to bond the coping-stones together.

Variations

There are certain jobs that will require a retaining/double-skin wall feature. An enclosure wall built on a weak soil bank, for example, will soon collapse. The ideal solution is to retain the bank and construct a stock-proof boundary at the same time. Mixing the retaining and double-skinned wall styles together can provide a feature that will have this dual function.

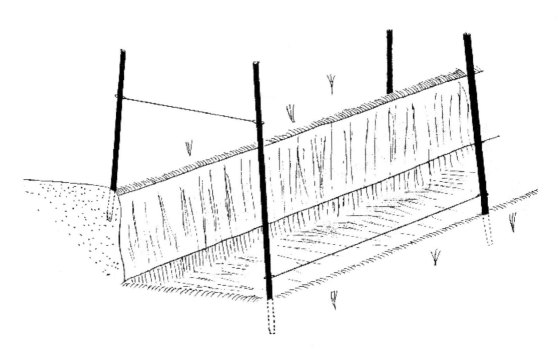

On a wall of this type it is easier to use four metal rods as opposed to normal batter-frames.

Batter-frame for a combined retaining and double-skinned wall.

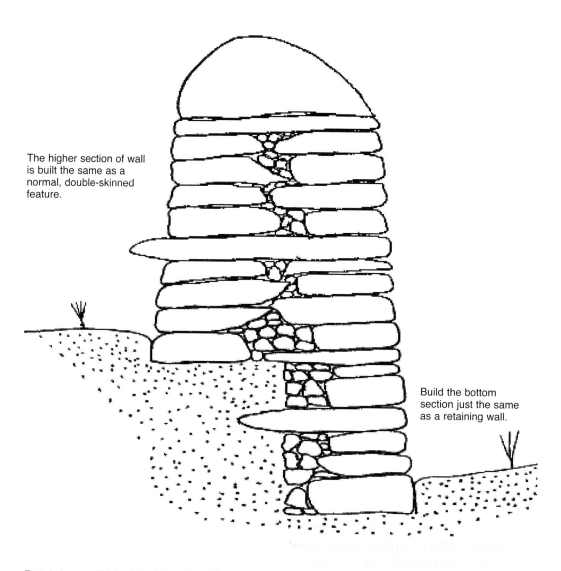

The higher section of wall is built the same as a normal, double-skinned feature.

Build the bottom section just the same as a retaining wall.

Retaining wall / double-skinned wall feature.

CHAPTER 9

ADVANCED WALLING

Special features are built into walls to provide useful and essential utilities within the countryside environment. These include: stiles for hikers or farm workers, access points that allow small livestock to cross from one enclosure to the other, sometimes called *hog-holes* although the name can vary depending on the local region (*see* Glossary for name variations).

Stiles

A wall crossing the definitive line of a public footpath will need to have some form of access to allow the public through. It is against the law to obstruct an existing public right of way and failure to maintain reasonable access can lead to a hefty fine or, in the extreme, a prison sentence. If you think there may be a footpath running through your land or, in some cases, your garden, consult the Footpaths Officer within your local authority. He or she will usually work for the Highways Department. All public rights of way are recorded on a document called the *Definitive Map*, with each path, bridleway or green lane designated an identifying number. Although the local authority is responsible for maintaining these paths it is up to the landowner to

make sure they are clear of obstructions. Bear in mind also that the proposed stile will have to be accurately sited on the path's definitive line (the official route of any public right of way). Again, the Footpaths Officer can help on this matter.

There are three practical ways to create access through or over a dry stone wall: a *stone step-over stile*, a *squeeze stile* or a wooden *ladder stile*. The first two are more in keeping and will last as long as the wall. The ladder stile, which this book does not cover, is the most expensive and will eventually need replacing due to user wear and tear, and wood rot.

To construct a stone step-over stile at least two through-stones, of around 3ft (90cm) in length, will have to be inserted through the wall in order to create a small flight of steps or *treads* on either side. To enable comfortable safe passage over the wall, each step will need to protrude at least 12in (30cm) from both faces of the wall.

Suitable-sized stone can be purchased from a quarry, but this could prove expensive on a limited budget. In the Peak District National Park most stone step-over stiles are built using concrete kerbstones. This is because around 80 percent of the footpaths cut across dry stone walls and implementing a strategy with natural stone is not cost effective. Another reason is that the material within the southern, limestone area is not long enough to create a safe passage over a wall. The preferred option, of course, is to use natural stone when it is available, but kerbstones are fairly inexpensive and can be purchased from most large builders' merchants.

Some regions do have a strict policy on using natural stone but it is usually where the local rock lends itself to the ideal size. Slate is perfect for this, as it can be split from the bedrock in large chunks.

If the proposed stile is part of the public right of way network, it may be worth talking to the local authority's Footpath Officer. As discussed earlier, it is his or her responsibility for maintaining rights of way and the authority may have a ready supply of suitable kerbstones – especially if their area includes a high proportion of dry stone walls. Only contact the local authority if the stile is going to be situated on a public footpath. They are not responsible for dealing with stiles built only for private access.

To add a stone step-over stile, part of the wall will need to be taken down in the shape of a reversed apex. Start by removing a 6–8ft (1.8–2.4m) length of coping and place the stones on one side. Look at

A stone step-over stile in a limestone wall. (Built by volunteers.)

The shaded stones represent the area to be removed.

The wall taken down in a step fashion.

Construction stages of a stone step-over stile – part 1.

Flat, top tread with mortared coping.

Treads must be level and parallel.

For safety, the treads can sit on a bed of mortar. For the centre of the wall use a mixture of mortar and hearting.

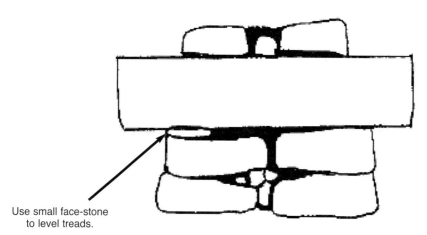

Use small face-stone to level treads.

Construction stages of a stone step-over stile – part 2

both faces of the wall, inspecting how the face-stones bridge the joins and work out how best the stone can be removed to form steps on either edge. Take the wall down one course at a time, making sure that each step is secured (*see* Chapter 5 for creating safe steps).

If the wall is strong it will only need to be taken down to within two courses of the foundation. If, on the other hand, the stone within the structure is badly weathered it should be removed down to the foundation stones.

The tops of the treads should be no more 12in (30cm) apart, otherwise traversing the wall could be difficult. The first tread can usually be placed on top of the first course. Once in position it can be manoeuvred so its point of balance is directly over the centre of the wall. Check its horizontal path with a spirit level and adjust as necessary by adding small face-stones underneath. For added strength and safety, some local authorities bed the treads and the surrounding stones in mortar. Although not in keeping with the philosophies of dry stone walling, this is an acceptable compromise where the safety of the public has to be taken into account. Colouring solutions can be added to the mortar to help it blend with the local stone, but in most cases they are not used. Add three parts sand to one part cement to form a strong bond.

Build up any gaps at the sides of the tread then place a course of stone on top, bridging the joins of the tread and the wall either side of the gap. Fill the wall's centre with hearting and lay a further course of stone, adding mortar if required. Place further courses until the second tread can be inserted (remembering that the tops of the two treads should

be about 12in (30cm) apart). Secure this tread like the first and then build the wall up to the top course of face-stone.

The actual crossing point of the stile will need to be directly above the second tread, leaving a 12–15in (30–40cm) gap in the coping to allow safe passage for the user. On most stiles this part of the structure is strengthened by a flat coping-stone, spanning the width of the wall and binding the two faces together. If one cannot be found employ a mortared, crazy-paving arrangement.

Replace the coping-stones, using the method described in Chapter 4, leaving a 12–15in (30–40cm) gap above the second tread. Most walkers, when climbing a stile, will pull themselves up, holding onto the coping. With this in mind, each of the three coping-stones on either side of the crossing point should be bedded in mortar and pointed up in-between.

On walls higher than 4ft 6in (1.4m) it is advisable to use three treads instead of two, for safe passage over the wall. If a three-treaded stile is built on a public footpath, or any public area, it is a health and safety requirement to place the treads at equal intervals apart. Where the ground is higher on one side, a *launcher-stone* can be bedded into the ground on the lowest side as a first tread.

Squeeze stiles are only effective in enclosures containing large livestock and, in some cases, adult ewes or in areas where stock proofing is not a priority. They are somewhat inadequate as a barrier for an inquisitive lamb or a goat bent on escape.

This type of stile is rarely built nowadays, with most work carried out on the repair of existing ones. Where a footpath cuts across an existing wall, the preferred option is to add a stone step-over stile. They are a better stock-proof device and less labour intensive to implement. A squeeze stile requires a wall to be dismantled to its foundations and then the assembling of two, strong wall-ends.

Adding a squeeze-stile during the construction phase of a new wall may be an alternative if ideal, stone treads cannot be found. The stile should consist of two, strong wall-ends of around 15in (40cm) apart (*see* Chapter 4 for the technique for building wall-ends). For added strength, the end-stones can be mortared in. This will stop livestock or walkers from disturbing the stone as they pass through. A more common alternative is to initially dig two large stone pillars into the ground, at roughly the same height of the wall, and then to build dry stone wall-ends against these. If this method is going to be used, make sure it is the stone pillars that are 15in (40cm) apart and not the wall-ends.

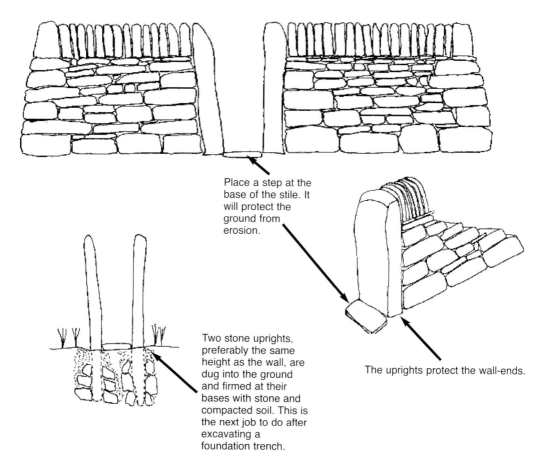

Place a step at the base of the stile. It will protect the ground from erosion.

Two stone uprights, preferably the same height as the wall, are dug into the ground and firmed at their bases with stone and compacted soil. This is the next job to do after excavating a foundation trench.

The uprights protect the wall-ends.

Squeeze stile.

Adding a Hog-Hole

A hog-hole is a small thoroughfare built into the bottom of a wall allowing small livestock free access from one enclosure to the other, whilst containing large animals such as cattle. A sheep farmer will use one when working with a sheep dog, for the dog will use the hog-hole instead of causing damage by jumping a wall.

Like squeeze stiles, hog-holes should really be built when a wall is under construction. All a hog-hole requires are two wall-ends, built to a height of at least 2ft (60cm) and a maximum width of 2ft (60cm), bridged at the top by two stone lintels with the higher section of wall constructed in the normal way (*see* Chapter 4 for building wall-ends and placing face-stones).

A hog-hole can also be useful for bridging intruding tree roots or a stream.

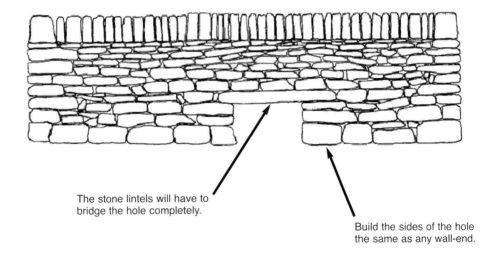

The stone lintels will have to bridge the hole completely.

Build the sides of the hole the same as any wall-end.

Try to avoid large spaces, where hearting can fall through the wall, between the lintels.

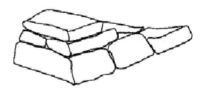

Hog-hole.

A hog-hole, note the two wall-ends and the lintels. (Constructed by students at Walford College.)

CHAPTER 10

VARIATIONS OF THE CRAFT

As discussed earlier in the book, dry stone walling follows a series of fundamental techniques, which are basically the same regardless of the style of wall. The methods described in this chapter consist of some advanced working practices and are easier achieved once the basic principles are attained. The various styles of wall throughout Britain show us just how fascinating and enjoyable this art form can be.

Some areas in Britain have produced their own methods of construction, which on first glance appear totally divergent from the projects described in this book. The Devonshire and Cornish forms of the craft are actually called hedges, although these areas do host the more traditional dry stone wall. Before attempting to build these it is advisable to seek out recognized training bodies and associations and enrol on one of the many well-run courses throughout the UK. In the appendix, there is a list of training establishments that can give advice on what they have on offer.

To whet your appetite, the following are a few examples of what can be achieved with a fair degree of knowledge and skill.

Cornish and Devon Hedges

These boundaries consist mainly of an earth wall, faced with natural stone and finished with either a turf *crown* or planted hedgerow species such as hawthorn and hazel. These are fascinating structures, but tend to be susceptible to erosion and require a higher degree of maintenance compared to a standard dry stone wall. Although very similar to the *Welsh Clawdd* (pronounced Clawth) this particular style is unique to the West Country. A few theories have been bandied about as to why this peculiar form of walling came into being. It is thought they were erected this way to create shelter for livestock in severe weather conditions or for raising the hedgerow from areas with a high water table to prevent the roots from becoming waterlogged.

As with any dry stone wall, the hedge will need to sit on a firm foundation. Working with the largest stones available, place these in a trench of around 5in (12cm) in depth and about 2.5–3ft (75–90cm) in width. With this style of walling the foundation stones sit at an angle, sloping into the wall. It is absolutely essential to make sure that all of the stone is placed with its length into the wall regardless of size. Instead of filling the centre with hearting, compacted soil or soil mixed with small rubble is used. The preferred hearting should be granular earth, if available.

To seal the wall at each end, construct normal wall-ends as described in Chapter 4.

Once the foundations are in and the soil or soil/rubble mixture in the centre is compacted, the intermediate courses can be built. As with the standard wall, build both sides of each course before starting on the next layer. Use a batter-frame to guide the wall to the correct batter. Rough-faced stones can be placed on their edges as long as their lengths are laid into the wall's centre. If large flat stones are available lay them horizontally, just like on a standard wall. This will help bind the smaller stones. Above all, make sure every stone, on each side of the wall, touches its immediate neighbour. This helps to lock the whole structure together.

Pay particular attention to the wall-ends. If the ends are not secured properly in accordance with method given in Chapter 4 they could collapse, allowing the elements to wash away the centre. Use the soil to fill the centre and compact it down, making sure that every gap behind the stones is filled.

The feature that sets this wall apart from any other is its concave section halfway up. This is where the wall appears to straighten once it has reached a height of around 3ft (90cm). Without delving into the complexities of physics, the concavity helps to disperse the weight downwards thereby adding strength to the finished product.

Instead of finishing the wall with coping-stones, the traditional method is to use turf, mounded to form what is called the crown. Some of these walls are built with a stone coping and these are usually placed on the top courses with their largest mass lying on the wall – just like a retaining wall. The general rule of thumb is to follow the exact style of the surrounding field boundaries. As explained in the early chapters, in conservation areas and national parks, this is a statutory requirement.

Welsh Clawdd

Like the Scottish walls, the Welsh forms of the art are called dykes. Although in Wales the majority of field walls are of very similar design to those built elsewhere in Britain, one particular style, the Clawdd, resembles the Devonshire and Cornish hedge. Building one of these to the correct specification requires a highly advanced technique, a very satisfying one if one can gain the skills to proceed with it. Although most are built to a height of around 3ft 3in (1m) they can, in fact, be raised as high as required to form an ideal field boundary. Unlike the Devonshire and Cornish walls, the Clawdd is usually constructed without the concavity beyond the halfway stage of construction. They are, however, slightly wider in form and require a substantial amount of compacted, granular soil.

A Clawdd sits in a foundation trench of around 5in (12cm) in depth. The width of the base may vary, but in practice it should be around 4ft 3in (1.3m) wide. Like all walls, a dual course of large stones is laid either side of a foundation trench. The centre should be filled with

Face-stones on this style of wall are placed so that they lean into the wall. This makes absolutely sure that the weight is forced into the centre.

When each course is complete fill the wall's centre with soil/rubble. Compact it down using a sledge hammer or tamper, making sure that every cavity behind the face-stones is filled.

On this cross section the wall has been planted with hedgerow species. The deep well of soil between the stones enables the root system to penetrate downwards. This stops them from disturbing the face-stones.

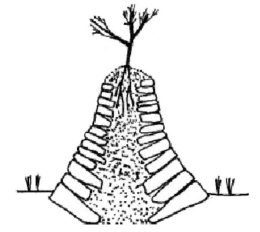

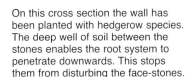

Cornish and Devonshire hedge.

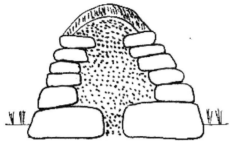

To create the dome at the top of the wall, shape and tamp the soil with the back of a shovel.

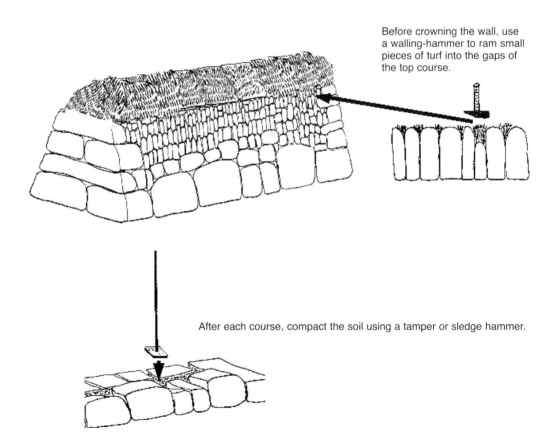

Before crowning the wall, use a walling-hammer to ram small pieces of turf into the gaps of the top course.

After each course, compact the soil using a tamper or sledge hammer.

Welsh Clawdd.

soil/rubble and compacted down, making sure that all gaps behind the stones are filled.

The size of the walling stones can vary, but they must be placed with the length running into the centre. As a general rule of thumb, the area of stone laid into the centre should be twice the face height. For example, if a walling stone has a face height of 5in (12cm) then, ideally, its length should be no less that 10in (24cm).

The same rule of laying one course of stone at a time applies to this wall. It is vitally important to make sure that all the stones on the face are butted up tightly to their immediate neighbours. Where the walling material is small, it is advisable to lay small sections then fill the centre with compacted soil. This will alleviate any possibility of collapse as you work down the course.

Stones are generally placed on their edges. If large stones are available they are best laid with their greater surface area on the wall. With all stone, make sure that the joins are crossed. To firm the courses even further, small stones called locking stones are rammed downwards into the gaps on the top of each course. All gaps underneath the stones should be pinned in the normal way to prevent movement.

Before finishing with a turf crown, small pieces of turf are rammed into the joints of the very top course to bind these stones together. Usually a 3ft 3in (1m) high Clawdd has a top width of 2ft (60cm). This allows room to plant hedgerow species such as hawthorn and hazel. If it is to be left without a hedge top, then a domed crown of turf is used to seal the wall together.

Once complete, the top of the Clawdd

should be protected against grazing from sheep or cattle. A wire fence, used as a temporary measure until the crown has matured, should be inserted along its entire length.

Limestone Walls (Cotswolds and White Peak)

The most striking features around the Cotswold countryside and the southern area of the Peak District National Park, known as the White Peak, are the limestone walls, which form their field boundaries. Limestone walls take considerably longer to erect than other styles and at the best of times it is a difficult material to work with. The friction bonding between each stone is far less than that of gritstone or slate and dressing this rock to a workable size can sometimes be a hit and miss affair, especially where the stone is old and has become brittle due to years of weathering. Virgin quarry-stone, by nature, is softer, therefore easier to work to shape using a walling hammer. Having said this, dressing limestone is an advanced technique, but to a highly skilled limestone waller this does not pose much of a problem and many of the Cotswold and Peak District walls are comprised of tight fitting, dressed stone.

Working with new limestone requires a large amount of hammer work in order to create a smooth base for walling. This is due to the many knobs and bulges as a result of the fossils contained within the rock. A further problem is that this type of stone, more so in the Cotswolds, is inclined to be too small when the need for through-stone arises. Many limestone walls are built using three-quarter throughs – stones that bridge the hearting and just touch the back of the opposite face.

Building a sturdy limestone wall requires a high degree of experience and it is not a job for the novice to rush headlong in to. However, as with all the techniques throughout Britain, the basic principles remain the same and a competently skilled individual should be able to erect an acceptable stock-proof structure.

Over much of the limestone country in Britain the soil strata tends to be quite thin. This is more exaggerated in the Cotswolds where the bedrock can be found as little as 3in (8cm) below the surface. Many walls in this region rest in shallow trenches upon this rock. If this base is uneven, great care should be taken when laying the foundations. An experienced craftsman will have no trouble in finding the ideal object to fit a disproportionate section of bedrock, or dress new quarry-stone to the correct shape. The inexperienced will undoubtedly find this type of ground highly frustrating to work on. Pinners must be diligently placed under all the gaps so that each stone becomes an independent, solid entity. Any movement of the wall will occur from the first course you lay and not the bedrock; a fact that has to be born in mind considering the majority of the foundation course will be above ground level.

The White Peak can be more forgiving and, more often than not, a suitable foundation trench can be excavated, unless you are working near the edge of a limestone escarpment where centuries of weather erosion have thinned out the loam.

As the majority of White Peak walls are built to a height of between 4ft 6in and 5ft 6in (1.4m–1.7m), the foundation trench should be excavated to roughly the same dimensions described in Chapter 4. In the Cotswolds the vast majority of boundary walls only reach a height of 3.3ft (1m) from base to coping, with the bottom width no more than 2ft (60cm) at most. Like all walls, the largest possible stones are used for the entire length of the foundation course, trimming off any irregularities with the chisel end of the walling hammer. It is important to make sure that the pinners are not disturbed when filling the centre with hearting.

Building the wall-ends can be quite a tricky affair when working with limestone; therefore I have added further text describing these at the end of this section.

The batter of a White Peak wall is more or less the same as the one constructed in Chapter 4, so the batter-frame and string-lines can be set up in accordance with this. The Cotswold walls, being fairly small in height, are built to a slightly different dimension. As previously explained, the base of the wall is 2ft (60cm) and the top width is usually no more than 14in (36cm).

The nature of random limestone is such that the majority of building stone comes in a triangular shape. Many have probably heard the saying, 'building a dry stone wall is like putting the pieces of jigsaw puzzle together'. Where this may not be entirely true when building in slate or grit stone, it is fair to say that the description is apt when working with limestone. Angled joins are not uncommon and finding the ideal stone to fit an angular gap can be a headache for the novice waller. This type of stonework is prevalent in the White Peak. As the area falls within the jurisdiction of the Peak District National Park Authority, any gapping or new walls will have to be built in harmony with the surrounding area.

Before laying the intermediate courses it is a good idea to allow some time to take a close look at the stone available. Make a conscious note of their differing sizes and shapes. If possible group all similar looking articles together; it may save time and patience when that awkward, only-one-stone-will-fit gap appears, as it invariably will on numerous occasions.

As ever, lay an entire course before starting on the next level. Where possible, try to choose stone of a similar height for each course, starting with the larger ones at the bottom, and decrease them in size as the wall is built to coping level. Use the latter advice as guide only. It is not uncommon for a limestone wall to host differing sizes of rock on any given course. However, common sense dictates that heavy stones should be laid somewhere near the foundation courses, otherwise the wall will become top heavy and liable to fall over.

Due to the stone's low friction, exceptional care must be taken to protect the pinners when filling the wall's centre with hearting. Cautiously place the small stones by hand around the back of the face-stones. Fill the centre level with the lowest stones on the course.

The procedure for finding the right face on the stone is exactly the same as on any dry stone wall. The front of the face-stones should slope away from the centre of the wall to divert the flow of rainwater to the ground either side. The stones should sit horizontal to the course, allowing a secure base for the row of stones above.

A course of three-quarter throughs can be laid when the wall has reached the halfway point.

Rectangular-shaped throughs on a limestone wall are a rarity. In keeping with the rest of the wall, the majority of the stone tends to be triangular. These should be laid with their narrowest end projecting towards the centre. If a smooth face can be achieved it is a bonus, but aesthetics may have to be compromised for the sake of the finished wall's stability.

When building up the wall-ends the small size of this stone poses a problem. The standard technique of crossing one through-stone on two runners can rarely be achieved on the lower courses of the wall. To overcome this dilemma a method of laying two stones on three is used rather than the usual two-on-one. Again, the aesthetic quality of the wall may have to be forfeited for the sake of its strength. If the material is fresh from the quarry a skilled waller will be able to carefully dress this stone to fit. Beyond the halfway point, as the wall batters in, finding decent sized through-stones should not pose a problem.

The size and shape of the coping is mainly dictated by the quality of stone available. The tops of many limestone walls are laid with stone of differing shapes and sizes. This invariably means that the coping-stones will look uneven when viewed from the front or down the line of the wall. The uneven effect can be reduced if a little time is taken to make sure that the very top of the wall is level. Building small sections of wall underneath the coping can raise the wall to an even height. It is important to bear in mind that each coping-stone must be secured with pinners, tightly locked together and cross the two faces to prevent the wall from falling apart.

Single-Skinned Walls

Up to now it has been apparent that most dry stone walls are built with two skins or faces. I am now going to throw a spanner in the works. For this particular section the 'Golden Rules' will be put to one side and consideration given instead to one of the strangest styles of wall Britain has to offer.

Although single-skinned walls account for only a minute percentage of the total length of walling in the British Isles, they are quite common in certain isolated areas of Dartmoor, Wales, Northern England and Scotland. They were mainly constructed in inaccessible mountainous regions where the delivery of quarry-stone was virtually impossible. The materials were lifted from the immediate terrain and, regardless of size, grouped together to form effective enclosures of around 3–4ft (90–120cm) high. Most walls were constructed out of igneous rock such as granite. Granite is practically impossible to break or dress with normal walling tools and this is the main reason why much of the stone in a single-skinned wall is very large.

Rebuilding or constructing a new wall is a task for a craftsman experienced in this particular field, as a high degree of skill is needed to build a single-skinned wall to an acceptable, safe standard.

A foundation trench should be excavated to minimum depth of 6in (15cm). Any soft areas inside the trench can be made firm by compacting small stone into the soil until the ground becomes hard. Single-skinned walls have no standard width at their base; this depends on the size of stone available – but the wider the foundations the higher the wall can be built. With this in mind, the waller should try to work to a width of around 2ft 6in (75cm) or wider. This will bring the height of the wall to 3ft 3in (1m) at least. The wall's viability as a stock-proof structure will be severely limited if built any lower.

All of the foundation stones should be laid across the trench in the same way one places throughs. They should be carefully manoeuvred so they are able to sit on their flattest and widest sides. The size of these foundation stones can pose a problem. In some cases they are so huge that it may take three or four people to manipulate them into position.

Due to the fact that these stones are difficult to manipulate once they are laid in the trench, every effort should be made to make sure that they will be able to abut their neighbours before laying them on the ground. Each stone is then levered with crowbars to close the joins and pinners are forced underneath with a hammer, not at the back of the stone like most walls, but under the side that has been lifted – similar to the method used for pinning coping-stone. It is also important to make sure that the pinning-stone does not raise the height of the foundation excessively, but merely acts as a wedge between the ground and the wall. At all times, it is the main stones that should bear the brunt of the weight.

Apart from a good technique, the durability of a double-skinned wall relies mostly on its two skins and the manner in which face-stones are laid. This is not an option on a single-skinned wall, so building up the courses requires a totally different technique. Like all walls it will still need two solid wall-ends but the usual method of crossing one-on-two cannot be applied. This will mean that the stones neighbouring the end-stones must be roughly the same height to enable the course on top to cross the join without the wall becoming unstable.

In some cases the end-stones lean slightly into the wall, a method that is repeated on the higher layers. This compresses the face-stones together, enhancing the weight dispersion down the entire length of the wall.

Keep laying the stone in this manner until the course is one stone away from the other wall-end. For this gap, a stone or stones that can be firmly slotted in to create a tight bond with the end-stone should be found. For the course as a whole, it is going to be impossible to find material of the same length and height. It is pointless to pay much attention to aesthetics, as all that will be created is a solid base to work on. It is essential, however, that the foundation course and all proceeding courses are as equal in width as possible, relative to their height on the wall.

Although this is a single-skinned wall, it will still have to be built with a batter to aid weight displacement. This can be achieved by choosing similar stones for each course, and then decreasing their size and width as it gets higher. On no account build the upper courses wider than the ones below, the wall will become top heavy and be liable to premature collapse.

Similar to the foundation, the two end-stones should be large enough to create a heavy solid tie and be able to bridge the join with the next stone along. There are two ways the face-stones can be placed on the wall. An odd-shaped stone can actually be slotted in vertically. Rectangular material, with flat sides, can be laid horizontal, but this type of stone may be short in supply. This being the case, it is advisable to alternate the stone so that each course is built with a mixture of horizontal and vertical pieces.

The face-stones should be secured in exactly the same way as the foundation course, with each stone forced against existing material. Pinners can be pushed in by hand, but they must fit flush with the stone. If they protrude they could cause the next stone to wobble. As on a double-skinned wall, each join will have to be bridged. With this style of wall, the joins between the stones will more than likely form a succession of 'V' shapes across its entire width. Laying face-stones inside these gaps, but still making sure that they can fit snugly against their neighbours, will form effective, staggered bonds as the wall reaches coping height.

The only time a string-line can be used to any effect is to provide a height guide for the coping. In keeping with the rest of the wall, coping-stones should be heavy and laid into the grooves created by the lower course.

This style of wall was added to the book to serve as an example of the durability of building without mortar. Constructing single-skinned walls requires skills beyond the basic principles outlined in previous chapters. For the well being of the general public, this style of wall should be left to the craftsmen who can build them to the safest possible standard.

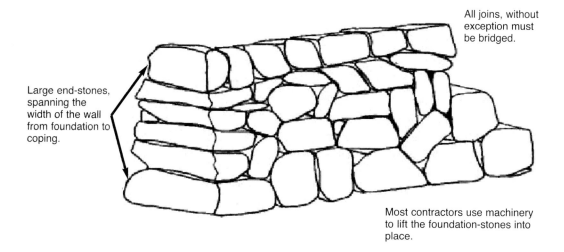

All joins, without exception must be bridged.

Large end-stones, spanning the width of the wall from foundation to coping.

Most contractors use machinery to lift the foundation-stones into place.

If built correctly a single-skin wall could last as long as any standard dry stone wall. However, the complexity of the construction technique really means that it is not a project for the inexperienced waller to take on.

Single-skinned boulder wall.

CHAPTER 11

A NATURAL STONE GARDEN

This chapter is not an in-depth guide to designing and creating a garden, but serves as a further example of the versatility of dry stone construction. This book, on the whole, has centred around working in the countryside. The reason is that this is where the majority of dry stone walls are found and the structures built or repaired there have all served a useful purpose within this environment. The majority of us, however, reside in urban areas where the chance to build a dry stone wall is severely limited.

The majority of new structures within the cities and towns are constructed utilising modern materials, but the older buildings including churches and some municipal facilities still proudly reveal the skilled, dressed faces of natural stone. One could be forgiven for thinking that a dry stone wall within these districts would appear lost and out of place, only waiting for the next developer to replace it with a straight, brick wall or palisade fence. This maybe true, but as part of a traditional garden theme a dry stone wall comes into its own, whether it be in the city centre or perched on the side of a mountain surrounding some sleepy, ancient cottage.

As a professional landscape gardener, my personal feelings toward the shape and feel of garden are biased on the side of the countryside. After all, isn't this the ultimate purpose behind a garden? A miniature fragment of the rolling hills and shaded woodland within easy reach of our back doors, a secure space for one to unwind and lift the stresses of everyday life, if only for a fleeting, special moment. A garden, to all intense and purposes, is our own private shred of customised, countryside indulging our individual needs and desires, specifically designed to create the peace and freedom only nature can offer.

A relaxing garden is one that can transport me to the serenity of a mountainous lakeland, adorned with sylvan and floral architecture, a place where the elements of nature entwine to form a myriad of special, private moments. Unfortunately a grandiose theme such as this can only be achieved if you are lucky enough to own a Scottish island or an entire mountain range, but the symbolism of this paradise can easily be transposed to fashion any garden plot large and small, city centre or otherwise.

The following photographs depict one of my completed garden projects. It is a theme based on natural stone retaining walls, combining to form a central water feature, complete with mountain stream

Artificial mountain stream constructed using dry stone walling techniques.

and slate patio area. Whilst this feature expands a large area, elements of this design can be custom-made to suit any plot.

Hidden from view, a butyl pond liner laid over a cushioning layer of sand forms a strong watertight base. Unseen, behind the retaining wall in the foreground, a breezeblock wall was constructed to act as a first barrier of defence to cushion the weight of water pushing up against the sides. The dry stone wall was added as an aesthetic shell. To further strengthen the sides of the pond, the wall was back filled using mortar and tied into the breeze-block with metal pins. As the photograph shows, this in no way detracts from the overall appearance of the feature.

The retaining wall sweeps round to form a revetment, which has helped to secure a natural stone, patio area. The flat, coping-stones were mortared into

position because of the heavy use that the garden was going to sustain.

A powerful, pump forces water from the pond to the head of an artificial, butyl lined mountain stream. The stream then flows through and over strategically placed stone, creating the tranquil sounds of a babbling brook, until finally plunging back into the pool. Newly plant-ed alpine species grace an artificial mountainside where random shaped rocks have been embedded into the soil. Eventually these plants will spread, and hide the harsh edges of the stone.

Water attracts an abundance of wildlife, some of which are helpful to the gardener. The crevices created by the dry stone wall afford shelter and security for frogs and beneficial insects. The iron rail-ings were erected by the owner as a safe-ty barrier, an essential comprise where the security of children is paramount.

Dry stone retaining wall securing natural stone patio; note the coping stones are mortared to prevent them becoming dislodged under heavy use.

Completed water feature with railings added for safety as the garden will be used by young children.

USEFUL ADDRESSES

If you have enjoyed this book and would like to study the craft in more detail the following is a list of organizations, togeth- er with their contact details, that run training courses and can provide further information.

Volunteers and full-time staff undertaking a dry stone wall training course in the Peak District National Park.

Organizations

British Trust for Conservation Volunteers
(BTCV)
36 St Mary's Street
Wallingford
OX10 0EU

Tel: (0) 1491 821600
Registered Charity No. 261009

The BTCV is Britain's largest, volunteer, conservation body. They offer training courses on every aspect of practical conservation and work alongside local authorities, National Parks and industry (to name but a few) on practical conservation projects. This highly professional and well-organized body offers a range of conservation holidays both at home and abroad. The vast range of skills that can be practised through this organization is boundless. To find out about the BTCV in your local area use the contact address above.

The Dry Stone Walling Association
of Great Britain (DSWA)
PO Box 8615
Sutton Coldfield
B75 7HQ

Tel/fax: (0) 121 378 0493
E-mail: j.simkins@dswa.org.uk
www.dswa.org.uk
Registered Charity No. 289678

Serving the craft of dry stone walling throughout Britain – and beyond.

The Dry Stone Walling Association of Great Britain, founded in 1968, is a democratic, members' organization and a registered charity. There are branches in most upland areas of Britain. The DSWA currently has 1,200 members of whom 250 are professional wallers and dykers.

The Association works to promote all aspects of the craft of dry stone walling. This includes publication of an annual Register of Certificated Professional Wallers, a series of technical specifications, plus a leaflet detailing courses. DSWA operates the only tiered, crafts skills certification scheme in Britain that involves work being carried out in presence of examiners – the Craftsman Certification Scheme.

Peak Park Planning Board
Aldern House
Bakewell
Derbyshire
DE45 1AE

Contact: Pete Hardwick (Volunteers Organizer)

The Peak District National Park offers many volunteering opportunities. They run a number of conservation projects during the week and at weekends and offer the chance to learn new skills or enhance existing ones. Brunts Barn, their purpose-built volunteers' centre, is second to none and their highly trained full-time and part-time staff are always eager to pass on their skills and expertise.

Other National Park Authorities, Areas of Outstanding Natural Beauty (AONB), Local Authority-Run Country Parks and Local Colleges

All these authorities will have openings for volunteers, and many will have ranger-led events programmes, conservation projects and training courses. It is well worth contacting your nearest authority for details. Even if there are no official training days in place, they may respond positively to enquiries and arrange some events. The contact details can be found in the local telephone directory. Local colleges may run full-time and part-time rural skills training.

Dartmoor National Park Authority
Bovey Tracey
Newton Abbott
Devon
TQ13 9JQ

Tel: (0) 1626 832093

North Shropshire and Walford College
Baschurch
Shrewsbury
Shropshire
SY42 2HL

Tel: (0)1939 262100

Useful Websites

The following websites provide interesting information and news on current conservation/dry stone walling issues.

ADAS
www.adas.co.uk/index.htm

Common Ground
www.commonground.org.uk/

Council for National Parks (CNP)
www.councilfornationalparks.freeserve.co.uk/

Council for the Protection of Rural England (CPRE)
www.greenchannel.com/cpre/

Council for the Protection of Rural Wales (CPRW)
www.cprw.org.uk/Default.htm

The Countryside Agency (CA)
http://www.countryside.gov.uk/

Countryside Council for Wales (CCW)
www.ccw.gov.uk/

Department of Agriculture and Rural development for Northern Ireland
http://www.dani.gov.uk/

English Heritage
www.english-heritage.org.uk/

English Nature (EN)
www.english-nature.org.uk/

Farming and Wildlife Advisory Group (FWAG)
www.snw.org.uk/enwweb/fwag.htm

Historic Scotland
www.historic-scotland.gov.uk/

Ministry of Agriculture, Fisheries and Food (MAFF)
www.maff.gov.uk/maffhome.htm

National Assembly for Wales
www.wales.gov.uk/

Protection of Field Boundaries
www.publications.parliament.uk/pa/
cm199798/cmselect/cmenvtra/969/
96902.htm

Ramblers Association (RA)
www.ramblers.org.uk/

RIGS (Regionally Important Geological & Geomorphological Sites)
www.rigs.org.uk

Royal Town Planning Institute (RTPI)
www.rtpi.co.uk/advice/index.htm

Scottish Natural Heritage (SNH)
www.snh.org.uk/

Scottish Office
www.scotland.gov.uk/whatwedo.asp

Shell
www.shell.co.uk/flash/index.html

Welsh Historic Monuments
www.castlewales.com/cadw.html

Women's Institute (WI)
www.nfwi.org.uk/

GLOSSARY

A-frame, Batter-frame: A wooden device used as a guide for building a wall to the correct angle or *batter*.

Batter: The angle on which a wall is constructed.

Bolt hole: Small access point at the base of a wall for the purpose of catching rabbits.

Bridging joins: The process of crossing the joins of *face-stones* on a dry stone wall or mortared brick wall.

Crown: The top of a Devonshire hedge, Cornish hedge and Welsh Clawdd. Usually made of turf which is formed into a dome.

Dressed stone: Stone cut on all sides to form attractive faces.

Dressing stone: The act of cutting natural stone to any desired shape.

End-stones: Large stone used for constructing a *wall-end*.

Foundation stones, foundation, footing, footings: The base of the wall.

Gapping: The act of repairing a damaged section of wall.

Hearting, Harting, Infill, Rubble, Centre-Stones: Small stone used to fill the gaps in middle of the wall.

Intermediate stones, face-stones: Stones used to build the section of wall between the coping and foundation.

Line level: A small spirit level that can be hung from a string-line. Used as guide for laying accurate horizontal courses.

Lunkie, hog-hole, smoot, thirl, chawl hole, cripple hole: Access points through a wall which allow the passage of livestock or the shooting of game and vermin.

Pinning, pinning-stone, pinners, wedges: Small stone used for jamming at the back of *face-stones* to counter any movement.

Random walling: Undressed walling stone. Stone in its natural state. Phrase used by quarries to identify dry stone walling product.

Retaining wall: A single-skinned wall usually built to stop erosion on soil banks or river sides. Retaining walls can form attractive garden features around the sides of ponds and planting beds.

Runners: Long pieces of stone used for *wall-ends*.

Semi-dressed stone: Stone cut on one or two sides to form an attractive face.

Squeeze stile: An access point on a path usually built out of two stone lintels or two wall-ends.

Stone step-over stile: An access point on a footpath where walkers can cross the top of a dry stone wall without causing damage.

Stone treads: Large *throughs* inserted through a dry stone wall to act as steps for a *stone step-over stile*.

Through-band: The middle section of wall where the majority of stones used are *throughs*. The through-band ties the two faces of a wall together.

Thru stones, through-stones, thrus, throughs: Large stones which tie both sides of a wall together. Usually placed at 3–4ft (90–120cm) intervals along a course. Used also to bridge *runners* on a *wall-end*.

Top stones, toppers, cap stone, cappers, coping-stones, copeing-stones, coins: The row of stones on the top of a wall.

Wall-end, cheek end: A secure end of a dry stone wall.

Walling out: A phrase used to describe the act of placing a stone on a course and not leaving enough room to work on the other side.

Walling: The act of building a wall. The collective name for walling stone.

Weathered face: The angled, front face of a walling stone. Allows rain to wash away from a wall instead of inside.

Weathering: A word used to describe the process of decay of natural rock.

Wooden ladder stile: An access point over a dry stone wall consisting of two flights of steps.

INDEX